The Slow Book Revolution

THE SLOW BOOK REVOLUTION

CREATING A NEW CULTURE OF READING ON COLLEGE CAMPUSES AND BEYOND

Meagan Lacy, Editor

AN IMPRINT OF ABC-CLIO, LLC
Santa Barbara, California • Denver, Colorado • Oxford, England

Library of Congress Cataloging-in-Publication Data

The slow book revolution : creating a new culture of reading on college campuses and beyond / Meagan Lacy, editor.

pages cm

Includes bibliographical references and index.

ISBN 978–1–61069–715–6 (paperback) — ISBN 978–1–61069–716–3 (ebook)

1. Books and reading—United States. 2. Books and reading—Psychological aspects. 3. College students—Books and reading. 4. Reading (Higher education) 5. Libraries and colleges—United States—Case studies. 6. Readers' advisory services. 7. Reading promotion. 8. Critical thinking. 9. Slow life movement. I. Lacy, Meagan, editor.

Z1003.2.S58 2014
028′.9—dc23 2014020796

ISBN: 978–1–61069–715–6
EISBN: 978–1–61069–716–3

18 17 16 15 2 3 4 5

This book is also available on the World Wide Web as an eBook.
Visit www.abc-clio.com for details.

Libraries Unlimited
An Imprint of ABC-CLIO, LLC

ABC-CLIO, LLC
130 Cremona Drive, P.O. Box 1911
Santa Barbara, California 93116-1911

This book is printed on acid-free paper ∞

Manufactured in the United States of America

Contents

PREFACE

With the advent of the Internet and the development of Web 2.0, the term "information overload" has made its way into popular usage. But in the context of the library profession, this concept is hardly new. Librarians have always had to confront "too much information," and it has been *our job* to manage and disseminate it effectively. Overload sort of goes with the turf, and ADD, we accept, is an occupational hazard.

Fortunately, though, librarians tend to be curious creatures and so are not easily thrown by excessive sensory input. This trait is partly what makes us good at our jobs. Personally, if someone says anything that resembles a reference question—*Can men breast-feed? What makes a cream ale* a cream ale*? Who is Wallace Langham? What is the etymology of the word seal?*—then I am scrambling for my iPhone or my iPad or my iMac to find an answer. It's hard to be still and just *not* know. Similarly, mention or recommend a book to me, and I have already opened up my library's OPAC and reserved it so that I can add it to the piles and piles of library books already sitting on my shelves, and under my coffee table, and next to my bed, the *to-be-read-eventually* piles.

So, when I found myself sitting in my office, trying to eat a sandwich, respond to an email, and listen to my officemate *all at the same time*, nothing seemed particularly amiss. I was simply multitasking, doing what I always do, managing information. Of course, I do not remember what my officemate was telling me or what I was trying to write in my email. I *do* remember what kind of sandwich I was eating, but that is only because I really like food and also because I was getting crumbs *everywhere*. At any rate, what alarms me about this incident isn't that I cannot recall these details today but that I could not recall them even then, as in, *when they were happening*. At some point, probably when I was wiping the crumbs off my desk, it occurred to me that

I wasn't doing anything very well. I wasn't listening well. I wasn't writing well. I wasn't even eating well. *Maybe*, I thought, *I should slow down.*

* * * *

I first came across the idea of "Slow Books" while reading Maura Kelly's *Atlantic* blog post "A Slow-Books Manifesto."[1] In this piece, Kelly reflects on the success of the Slow Food movement, how followers boast that preparing and eating local, whole foods is not only healthier and more sustainable but also more pleasurable. Given Slow Foods' supporters, and the many other "slow" movements that have followed, Kelly wonders why a similar effort hasn't assembled to improve our intellectual health: "Why so much emphasis on what goes into our mouths, and so little on what goes into our minds. . . . Why hasn't a hip alliance emerged that's concerned about what happens to our intellectual health, our country, and, yes, our happiness when we consume empty-calorie entertainment?"[2] As a response, she suggests we read literature, that is, "works that took some time to write and will take some time to read."[3] Such works, she argues, sharpen our minds and our identities. They are a means with which to resist the fragmentation, passivity, and mindlessness induced by our increasingly technologically mediated lives.

Slow Book Revolution responds to Kelly's call to action. As the following pages will demonstrate, reading, in the slow, book-length sense of the word, is still relevant and important—not *in spite* of our speed-obsessed, always-on, digital culture but *because* of it. By prompting us to slow down and focus on a sustained line of thought, reading literature provides a joyful respite from these digital distractions. The sheer state of being so absorbed is in itself a pleasure, but the pleasures of reading go far beyond that. Reading feeds our imaginations, our creative impulse. It also entertains. And comforts. It provides a means with which we can expand our identities and beliefs and better understand those of others. Reading also helps us connect to others—to the author, to other worlds and cultures, and to other readers—and therefore has the power to bring communities together.

The following chapters discuss how libraries, particularly academic libraries, can help readers discover, or rediscover, these pleasures. As repositories of the print (and electronic!) word, libraries are ideally suited to this task. Through readers' advisory, book discussion groups, One Book reading programs, and more, libraries can tap into reading's social side and help to build real connections between people. Such community offers a refreshing change of pace from the virtual world, where the semblance of intimacy, "the illusion of companionship,"[4] tends to dominate.

This book is split into three parts. The first part establishes a rationale for the Slow Books movement. Chapter 1 compares online reading to slow reading and explains how Slow Books can counteract the problems associated with our always-on digital culture. Chapter 2 describes the history of readers' advisory in academic libraries to explain why they, in particular, need to make a more concerted effort to promote recreational reading and Slow Books.

Parts II and III of this book are a combination of case studies and advice. These chapters are written by librarians about their readers' advisory practice and so provide concrete guidance on ways to contribute to this movement. Part II focuses on academic libraries, as they have only recently started to take a more intentional role with regard to recreational reading promotion. Part III focuses on how academic libraries can partner with other institutions—public libraries, K–12 schools—to deepen the impact of Slow Books. Thematically, all of these chapters are linked in their insistence that readership is best encouraged through social support, which libraries can easily provide.

In Chapter 3, Pauline Dewan explains how academic libraries, through relevant collections, readers' advisory services, and inviting library spaces, can help students develop a lifelong reading habit. In Chapter 4, Harold Henkel shows how his book group, focused on "the great books," connects and supports *all* readers—students, faculty, and staff—to build a culture of reading on his campus. In Chapter 5, Julie Elliott explains how she used One Book, One Community programming to not only build community on her campus but also to complement the curriculum and to stimulate new interest in reading among students. In Chapter 6, Barbara Fister describes the reading courses that she has created and taught at Gustavus Adolphus College. By allowing students to explore their own reading preferences and by teaching them how to be their own readers' advisors, these courses not only encourage recreational reading but also offer excellent models for teaching librarians who are looking for alternative ways to impart information literacy skills to their students. In Chapters 7 and 8, Willie Miller and Elizabeth Brookbank share how libraries can draw on existing student communities, in residence halls and online, to better support a campus culture of reading. By adopting any one of these outreach activities, academic libraries send the message to students that recreational reading is also a part of their education and a condition to their lifelong learning.

Part III of this book identifies other partners with whom academic libraries can collaborate to expand the Slow Books movement into the broader community. In Chapter 9, Sarah Fay Philips and Emerson Case describe how they have included students from feeder high schools in Bakersfield, California, in their One Book, One Community program at California State University Bakersfield. One of the advantages of this collaboration is that students are exposed to literacy activities outside of the classroom and thus learn that reading is not *only* for school. At the same time, these programs introduce them to college-level reading and expectations, easing their transition from high school to college. In Chapter 10, Rebecca Malinowski gives advice for how public and academic libraries can partner to more effectively promote Slow Books programs and deepen their impact. Finally, in Chapter 11,

Evanston Public librarians Karen Hansen and Lesley Williams take the movement to its apotheosis. Adopting the theme "One Book. One Year. One Mission: Finish," they support and motivate readers as they work through a single difficult text or author through a yearlong book discussion.

In this way, *Slow Book Revolution* both embraces and reclaims libraries' traditional bookish image. After all, people continue overwhelmingly to identify libraries with books.[5] Why not capitalize on this perception to reiterate the value of reading in the digital age? It seems shortsighted to me to downplay the one thing that sets libraries apart from all other institutions—a wide selection of new and often rare, *free* books. Without books, and without people who know a lot about them, there isn't much to distinguish a library from a computer lab or a study lounge. Books are the library's soul. And while they might lack the trendy appeal of microblogging sites like Twitter and Tumblr, that doesn't mean they can't compete. They could be sold as the classic, never goes out of style little black dress instead of the spandex stirrup pants of the past. The issue is promotion, not relevance. Thus, this book provides all of the examples, imagination, and inspiration you need to promote slow reading and incite a Slow Book revolution at your library.

NOTES

1. Maura Kelly, "A Slow-Books Manifesto," *Atlantic* (blog), March 26, 2012 (8:03 a.m.), http://www.theatlantic.com/entertainment/archive/2012/03/a-slow-books-manifesto/254884/.
2. Ibid.
3. Ibid.
4. Sherry Turkle, *Alone Together* (New York: Basic Books, 2012).
5. Cathy De Rosa et al., *Perceptions of Libraries and Information Resources: A Report to the OCLC Membership* (Dublin, OH: OCLC Online Computer Library Center, 2005), 3–31.

Acknowledgments

I want to thank my editor, Barbara Ittner, for encouraging me to take on this project in the first place; the librarians at Indiana University–Purdue University Indianapolis who, for five years, nurtured and supported me like a family; the interlibrary loan staff for fulfilling so, so many requests for books and articles; Claire McQuerry, Willie Miller, Robert Rebein, Steve Towne, and Scott Weeden for reading and commenting on earlier drafts of my chapters; Mom and Dad; Emily, for possessing superior sloth drawing skills and also for loving me like a sister; and Zach for inspiring me to struggle for the "radiancy of better things."

PART I

Reasons to Go Slow

1

What Is Slow Books?

Meagan Lacy

Most Americans are not reading. At least, they are not reading in the literary, book-length sense of the word. The National Endowment for the Arts' often cited report, *Reading at Risk: A Survey of Literary Reading in America*, states that "less than half of the adult American population now reads literature."[1] Of those surveyed in 2002, only 46.7 percent claimed to have read a single novel, short story, poem, or play for pleasure during that year.[2] Of the respondents who were college aged (i.e., between the ages of 18 and 24), this number fell to 42.8 percent.[3] A follow-up report, *To Read or Not to Read* (2007), confirmed this trend, concluding, "Both reading ability and the habit of regular reading have greatly declined among college graduates."[4] Although these reports neglect to mention whether Americans are reading other kinds of texts—including blogs, Facebook, and other web-based content—they nonetheless get at the reality that literary reading is on the decline.

To complicate this problem, we have entered an "age of digital distraction."[5] Overwhelmed by devices that ring, vibrate, and beam—devices that, in other words, relentlessly demand attention and response—today's generation faces a unique set of challenges when it comes to reading. Basically, many of these children and young adults cannot concentrate long enough to do it. Wired for distraction, they struggle to maintain the focus that traditional reading requires. This problem manifests itself in schools and colleges across the country. For example, researchers at the Pew Internet Project found that teens' constant use of digital technologies was interfering with their learning and academic performance. Of the teachers surveyed, 87 percent agreed that these habits were creating an "easily distracted generation with short attention spans."[6]

Observers of both these trends have long feared their impact on our culture. Sven Birkerts sounded the alarm for reading almost a decade before the NEA findings, in 1994, before the word "smartphone" had even entered our vocabulary, when we had only television to blame for the death of the novel. In *The Gutenberg Elegies: The Fate of Reading in an Electronic Age*, he laments, "If a person turns from print—finding it too slow, too hard, irrelevant to the excitements of the present—then what happens to that person's sense of culture and continuity?"[7] After all, he adds, "Our entire collective subjective history—the soul of our societal body—is encoded in print."[8] For Birkerts, reading's decline spells the end of history, of humanity, as we know it. But how justified is this fear? Aren't new technologies always greeted with doubt and suspicion? Is the problem the electronic/information/digital age or Birkerts' stubborn resistance to embrace what is simply new and improved?

Certainly, many readers have found his response a tad too alarmist and pessimistic. Novelist Jonathan Franzen writes, "Birkerts . . . underestimates the instability of society and the unruly diversity of its members."[9] In other words, just because we use these new technologies does not mean that we no longer value reading or do not *want* to read traditional books. Neither does it mean that deep reading, even in the age of digital distraction, is no longer possible. Still, Birkerts was right to recognize that these new technologies, intent on speed, do not develop the habits, patience, and persistence that traditional reading requires. As David Mikics, author of *Slow Reading in a Hurried Age*, points out, "Book-length arguments and works of imaginative literature reveal themselves only over time."[10] But it is precisely for this reason that reading struggles to compete with other recreational activities.

These trends might be less upsetting if it were true that online reading were an equal substitute for reading books. But it isn't. Online reading practices disrupt, rather than encourage, reflection and critical thinking, capacities that are fundamental not only to one's academic success but also to economic and political security. Reading books, on the other hand, develops these capacities. It is one of books' unique functions. And while Internet technologies have brought unimaginable advancements and discoveries to both the sciences and the humanities, they cannot claim to have fully and effectively replaced this function. Consider, for example, that eReaders do not do much more than simulate the experience of reading an actual, physical book. So in the absence of a support in the present technologies for deep thinking, books and reading remain relevant and important. Perhaps even more so today than ever before. As novelist and editor of *Ploughshares* Ladette Randolph points out, "In a fast-paced world with more choices than we can possibly entertain, quiet contemplation has become the scarcest of resources."[11] A deliberate effort is needed to counteract this trend. Hence, Slow Books.

The Slow Books movement seeks to reacquaint readers with the pleasures of books and, particularly, literature. While acknowledging that such reading requires time and patience—*work*—it maintains that expending such effort is also the source of reading's pleasures. Mikics puts it in another way: "We must work hard to get more out of the books we read—and good books always reward slow-moving, careful attention."[12] Quiet contemplation *is* the reward of slow reading, although—clearly—not the only one. The act is an end in itself, a response to, and a way of counteracting, the fragmentation brought on by our increasingly mediated lives.

THE PROBLEM WITH ONLINE READING, OR "FAST READING"

While the Internet has increased the diversity of and ease of access to information—revealing its democratizing potential—the Internet has also transformed the way that we consume and manage it. The sheer quantity of information on the web has driven us to new practices of reading in which we scan and decode online texts to absorb relevant pieces of information very quickly. As we have developed these habits, our very consciousness has changed. Nicholas Carr famously describes this phenomenon in his *Atlantic* article "Is Google Making Us Stupid."[13] He starts by saying:

> Over the past few years I've had an uncomfortable sense that someone, or something, has been tinkering with my brain. . . . My mind isn't going—so far as I can tell—but it's changing. I'm not thinking the way I used to think. I can feel it most strongly when I'm reading. . . . I get fidgety, lose the thread, begin looking for something else to do. I feel as if I'm always dragging my wayward brain back to the text. The deep reading that used to come naturally has become a struggle.[14]

The problem, he suggests, is the medium. The computer, like every medium before it—the typewriter, the telephone, the television—is not merely an instrument that carries and delivers messages. It also influences how those messages are perceived. Marshall McLuhan made this observation famous by coining the phrase "The medium is the message."[15] The medium delivers content but also, by virtue of being the medium, becomes a part of it—shaping the meaning of the message and, by extension, the way that we think.

Developmental psychologist Maryanne Wolf offers a cognitive explanation for this phenomenon. In her beautiful book *Proust and the Squid*, she explains how writing, another technology, also came to change not only *how* we expressed our thoughts but also *what* we thought. In fact, "We were never born to read."[16] Rather, because of the brain's intrinsic, unique design, its plasticity, we were able to acquire this skill. In an essay, she adds, "Unlike vision or language, reading has no genetic programme that unfolds to create an ideal form of itself. Rather, learning to read lies outside the original repertoire of the human brain's functions and requires a whole new circuit to be built afresh with each new reader."[17] Put simply, becoming an expert reader requires practice—a deliberate shaping of the brain—so that those neurological structures that permit reading to become easy and virtually automatic can form. Wolf adds, "These circuits and pathways are created through hundreds, or in the case of some children with reading disabilities like dyslexia, thousands of exposures to words."[18] As these connections form, our brains literally change, and so does our thinking.

By freeing us from the constraints of an oral tradition that relied on memory and formulaic, mnemonic strategies, reading not only expanded the boundaries of expression but also what could actually be thought. Consider how reading a novel or other literary work will often provoke ideas that are not contained in the text itself. Anything—a character, an image, a word—might trigger an association that moves us from the page in front of us into our own imaginations. We do not merely re-create the author's thoughts. We reflect and go beyond them. This generative, creative quality is at the heart of reading, and it is what makes reading so important. "Within such a broadened context," Wolf explains, "there can be no surprise that one of the most profound and prolific periods of writing, art, philosophy, theater and science in all of previously recorded history accompanied the spread of the Greek alphabet."[19] Through writing, novel thought was more possible and more accessible. Although Socrates was highly critical of writing—in the *Phaedrus*, he fears its illusory quality, its susceptibility to manipulation, and its potential to "implant forgetfulness"[20] in learners' souls—it possessed clear advantages. Namely, the record: There would be no *Phaedrus* if Plato hadn't written it down. Furthermore, and even more importantly, writing created a new state of mind. Walter Ong explains that "Plato's philosophically analytical thought . . . including his critique of writing, was possible only because of the effects that writing was beginning to have on mental processes."[21] Science, history, philosophy, literature, music, and art would not have advanced to their present states without literacy. Again, writing—a technology—changed not only *what* we thought but also *how* we thought.

In the same way, the Internet, the biggest technology since the printing press, has also necessarily changed our brains and our thinking. In other words, the reason that Nicholas Carr feels like something has been "tinkering with his brain" is because quite literally something *has*. Overwhelmed by the sensory stimuli of the online environment, the brain *must* adapt to manage all of the information flickering on the computer screen. As a result, deep reading and sustained concentration become more difficult. Carr explains, "The need to evaluate links and make related navigational choices, while also processing a multiplicity of fleeting sensory stimuli, requires constant mental coordination and decision making, distracting the brain from the work of interpreting text or other information."[22] This extra cognitive burden is not totally unlike the burden experienced by ancient readers of *scriptura continua*, an early form of writing in which words ran together and lacked punctuation. The task of decoding individual words, of puzzling out the beginnings and ends of sentences, would have been a laborious task to say the least. But as writing evolved, "the placing of spaces between words alleviated the cognitive strain involved in deciphering text, making it possible for people to read quickly, silently, and with greater comprehension."[23] In other words, this added white space gave readers *time* to understand the text; it became a part of the composition and a part of its meaning.

Although Carr concedes that it is possible to "think deeply while surfing the Net, just as it's possible to think shallowly while reading a book," he also observes that neither is "the type of thinking the technology encourages and rewards."[24] Because reading online is so much more cognitively difficult than reading in print, we are encouraged to skim and scan, to gather the particulars but not peruse them. As a further complication, the more time that we spend skimming and scanning web pages rather than reading books, the more "the circuits that support those old intellectual functions and pursuits weaken and begin to break apart."[25] In other words, as our brain changes, it becomes harder to think in the old way, the deep way. The old neurological connections atrophy as our habits change. We train ourselves to be distracted: "Our brains become adept at forgetting, inept at remembering."[26] Although the new pathways allow us to process information quickly and efficiently, we remember and comprehend less. This situation begs the question: What happens to creativity, to culture, if the Google brain dominates? If the Internet encourages distracted thinking, if our capacities for sustained thought are not developed, how can creativity and innovation exist? Tech writer Edward Tenner expresses this same concern when he writes in a *New York Times* op-ed piece, "It would be a shame if brilliant technology were to end up threatening the kind of intellect that produced it."[27] Let's not forget: The brains that dreamed up Google were reading brains.

Michael Merezenich, renowned for his pioneering brain mapping research, states the problem even more succinctly: "When culture drives changes in the ways that we engage our brains it creates DIFFERENT brains," and the heavy use of online tools "HAS NEUROLOGICAL CONSEQUENCES."[28] Does this mean that we should issue every smartphone with a warning from the surgeon general? *Caution: Smartphone use may be hazardous to your health.* Or maybe a public service announcement? *This is your brain. This is your brain on the Internet . . . Any questions?*

THE SOLUTION: SLOW BOOKS

I am not recommending that we abandon our smartphones and iPads. In fact, I cringe a little whenever I hear someone joke about his or her willful ignorance of computers and technology. For one, we cannot pretend that this transformation hasn't already occurred. New technologies, once introduced, have a decisive effect on our culture. This is true of writing, and this is true of the web. As Carr says, "We cannot go back to the lost oral world, any more than we can turn the clock back to a time before a clock existed."[29] Or, as Walter Ong puts it, "Writing and print and the computer are all ways of technologizing the word. Once the word is technologized, there is no effective way to criticize what technology has done with it without the aid of the highest technology available. Moreover, the new technology is not merely used to convey the critique: in fact, it brought the critique into existence."[30] Recall that Plato's objections to writing are *written* in a dialogue. He correctly observes that the absence of the physical author/speaker makes ideas expressed in writing susceptible to misinterpretation and manipulation and also that reliance on writing diminishes memory. Nonetheless, he also recognizes that through writing, he is still able to carry out the tradition of deep thinking and philosophical thought that dialogue fosters. So although not all functions of orality can be replaced by writing, writing does not *inhibit* deep thinking but rather expands it.

In the present technological context, however, it is unclear what the replacement for deep thinking is going to be—or even if there will be a replacement. For these reasons alone, books and narrative-length reading remain relevant. By slowing us down and inducing a state of quiet and reflection, they reward and encourage deep thinking and sustained thought. In this way, books are a superior technology. By clarifying the position of books in our total information ecology, and by teaching readers how to navigate between technologies and to adapt their reading styles based upon their purpose—that is, finding information versus understanding it—we can teach the value of both. Wolf concludes in her book, "We must teach our children to be 'bitextual,' or 'multitextual,' able to read and analyze texts flexibly in different ways, with more deliberate instruction at every stage of development on the inferential, demanding aspects of any text."[31] It's not that one technology is better or worse—or that one technology ought to replace another—but simply the fact that a book serves a purpose that no other technology, as of yet, can replace. Understanding this difference is basic information literacy, ACRL Standard 1.2.c. to be exact: The information-literate student "Identifies the value and differences of potential resources in a variety of formats (e.g., multimedia, database, website, data set, audio/visual, book)."[32]

For this reason, librarians—more than anyone—are poised to lead the Slow Books movement. First, as teachers of information literacy, librarians are already teaching their users how to become multitextual. Second, as iconic symbols of the printed word, libraries possess the cultural cachet to change and transform attitudes toward reading. And this, to my thinking (as I do feel a synapse fire every now and again), is the only way that the book and its concomitant benefits—creativity and sustained, linear thought—can persist. As Fran Lebowitz comments in *Public Speaking*, "A very discerning audience, an audience with a high level of connoisseurship[,] is as important to the culture as [an] artist."[33] Libraries, as selectors and tastemakers, have the ability to create and mold that audience and therefore preserve a culture around reading.

The Commission on the Humanities and Social Sciences has also articulated this need to restore a culture of reading. Their report, *The Heart of the Matter*—which was commissioned by a band of four bipartisan lawmakers—argues and affirms that the humanities and social sciences are critical to the future of this country and to achievement of national goals. They write, "Today, our need for a broadly literate population is more urgent than ever. As citizens, we need to absorb an ever-growing body of information and to assess the sources of that information."[34] Alluding to a "broadly literate population," the commission echoes the same conclusions as Wolf about teaching students to become, flexible, multitextual readers. More than basic literacy,[35] they envision a population of readers able to evaluate, analyze, and synthesize texts of varying complexity—a population that is, in other words, information literate. For this reason, the commission specifically lists literacy as a fundamental twenty-first-century skill that is essential to a thriving democracy: "The nation depends on a fully literate populace—on citizens whose reading, writing, speaking, and analytical skills *improve over a lifetime* [my italics]. These are among the principal skills that the humanities and social sciences teach, and they must be nurtured *at every level of education* [my italics]."[36] Deep reading skills are a critical social capacity. Again, those who are not "fully literate," who cannot read or write *well enough*, are effectively disenfranchised—academically, economically, and politically. To nurture this population of readers, libraries can, as Maryanne Wolf suggests, provide instruction at *every stage of development*. This means that reading should be promoted among children, teens, young adults, and adults at school, public, *and* academic libraries.

Slow Books Defined

As mentioned earlier, the term "Slow Books" originates from Maura Kelly's *Atlantic* blog post titled "A Slow-Books Manifesto"[37] and builds on the same principles as slow food. In other words, Slow Books operates on the assumption that reading good literature, like eating good food, improves one's quality of life. Kelly's mantra "Read books. As often as you can. Mostly classics"[38] is meant to echo Michael Pollan's "Eat food, not too much, mostly plants."[39]

Since the publication of Kelly's blog post, others have called for similar movements, sometimes referring to them as slow reading instead.[40] Kelly, however, is not the first to draw this parallel. The idea of Slow Books, as a movement, may be new, but the philosophy underlying it has been percolating for some time. For example, John Miedema, who expanded his independent research on slow reading for his MLIS degree into a book entitled *Slow Reading* (2009), also borrows from the concept of slow food. He contrasts slow reading[41] with "fast books," that is, books that are "produced for the broadest possible appeal, stamped out in assembly lines and distributed at points of maximum exposure such as Amazon or warehouse-sized bookstores."[42] Like fast food, fast books tend to be bland, uninspired, and produced primarily for profit.[43] For these reasons, fast books threaten culture much like fast food threatens agriculture and the environment. As a response, Miedema advocates "local reading," that is, seeking out writers and places associated with local stories. Local reading, he says, "engages memories and feelings only a local resident will share."[44] It connects readers to their literary community and enriches their reading experience.

In his book, Miedema also draws distinctions between print and online reading practices. He concedes that online reading accommodates "our casual information needs."[45] By encouraging rapid scanning, it is useful for searching and reading snippets, that is, for quick information retrieval. But, he concludes, print is "the superior technology for slow reading anything of length, substance, or richness."[46] In other words, it is the superior technology for reading books, especially literature. This is a pointed claim coming from Miedema, who himself was employed as an information technology specialist at IBM at the time of his writing—it's not the sort of opinion one would expect from a person specializing in web technologies. He explains, "Like many people, I value digital search for finding quick answers and leads. . . . However, if the content I have found is anything longer than a few pages, or if it has any depth, I prefer to read it in print."[47] Although eReader technology has improved since *Slow Reading* was published, Miedema has a point. Print media are more conducive to slow reading than digital technologies simply because they are less likely to distract a reader. A printed book does not contain hyperlinks; it does not beep whenever a friend sends you a Facebook message or the *New York Times* sends you a news alert. Nonetheless, the Slow Books movement is *not* print prescriptive. As Kelly says, "The Slow Books movement won't stand opposed to technology on purely nostalgic or aesthetic grounds. (Kindles et al[.] make books like *War and Peace* less heavy, not less substantive, and also ensure you'll never lose your place.)"[48] Ultimately, the purpose of Slow Books is to encourage reading, whether in print or on an eReader.

Why? Because reading, like eating, is pleasurable. It provides relief from a frenzied, always-on lifestyle. The *Slow Food Manifesto*, signed in 1989 by representatives from 15 different countries, states, "A firm defense of quiet material pleasure is the only way to oppose the universal folly of Fast Life."[49] Slow books makes the same assumption. Its goal is to spread the pleasure of reading good books, *not* prescribe them as if they were medicine (e.g., "Books are good for you," "Reading is your duty"). The pleasure of quiet contemplation—what, remember, Ladette Randolph calls "a scarce resource"—is an end in itself.

Of course, part of what makes a meal pleasurable is choosing the menu. For Slow Books, choice matters, too. Miedema explains: "Applying a highly prescribed technique or forcing the reading in some way is contrary to the essence of slow reading; to some extent, it must be voluntary . . ."[50] The reader must be able to exercise choice about what he or she reads and at what pace. "This freedom," Miedema adds, "brings back the pleasure of reading."[51] It is for this reason that libraries are so well positioned to lead the Slow Books movement. Unlike most classroom settings, libraries provide readers with choices and allow them to follow the path of their own curiosity.

In his belief of the importance of voluntary reading, Miedema echoes Stephen Krashn, author of *The Power of Reading* (2004), and his notion of free voluntary reading (FVR). FVR, defined as "reading because you want to,"[52] plays a fundamental role in one's development as a reader. Krashn admits, "Nearly everyone in the United States can read and write."[53] The problem, though, is that "They just don't read and write well enough."[54] Thus, his solution for the literacy crisis is plainly to encourage reading, particularly FVR. He concedes, "I will not claim that FVR is the complete answer. . . . What the research tells me is that when children or less literate adults start reading for pleasure, however, good things will happen."[55] This list of "good things" includes improved reading comprehension, improved ability to read difficult academic-style texts, improved writing, improved vocabulary, and improved spelling and grammar. By itself, FVR may not produce the highest levels of reading competence, but it does provide a "foundation so that higher levels of proficiency may be reached."[56] So by promoting the pleasures of Slow Books, school, public, and academic libraries can tacitly address their educational objectives as well.

Leading the Slow Books Movement

Slow Books is primarily about promoting the pleasures of reading—reading that is exclusive of email, texting, instant messaging, Facebook, and anything limited to 140 characters. Promoting FVR is the first step. Already, public libraries excel at this, and for this reason, much of this book focuses instead on academic libraries and how they can borrow and adapt public libraries' readers' advisory practices. But the next step, for all kinds of libraries, is to make a more intentional effort to expand and develop readers' tastes by encouraging them to explore more complex literary texts and supporting them as they endeavor to do so. By "literary texts," I mean books that emphasize fine writing and that possess an artistic vision. Whether fiction or nonfiction, they employ literary techniques (e.g., complex characters, poetic language, rhythm, symbolism) to tell stories that probe the human condition.[57] In making this distinction, I do not mean to downgrade popular literature or to equate it to "fast food." Rather, I think a more apt comparison would be to dessert. Dessert is completely necessary to one's happiness (at least, I know it's completely necessary to *my* happiness), but no one's diet should consist entirely of it. It is the same with popular literature.

Literature is distinguished by the exceptional extraordinary effects it has on the reader. These effects are not supposed, but real. For example, Oatley, Zoeterman, and Peterson recently conducted an experiment in which they compared changes in participants' affect after reading Chekhov's short story "Lady with the Toy Dog" with changes in those who had read a factual account of the same story that was roughly the same length. The results revealed that people who had read the literary short story experienced significantly greater change in personality traits and emotions than the control group and that this difference appears to be linked to the powerful emotional response that the literary story evoked.[58] In other words, this research suggests that the emotions stirred by literature may alter, in subtle ways, peoples' personalities. In another recent study, Kidd and Castano report that reading literary fiction enhances one's capacities to identify and understand other's subjective states—that is, to empathize—more than reading nonfiction and popular genre fiction.[59]

To bring it back to slow food, part of the reason Carlo Petrini's movement was so successful was that he made people understand "taste is serious matter."[60] Sharing in the pleasures of good food has the power to draw individuals together who might not otherwise have anything in common. Petrini explains, "Taste buds are neither conservative nor liberal, and, though it may be impossible to change the world, one should at least be able to change the menu."[61] In the same way that the Arci Gola drew communities in Italy together through fine food, libraries have the power to draw communities together through fine books.

While some librarians may bristle at the mere mention of taste and fear that privileging literature in any way automatically degrades popular fiction, promoting Slow Books is not an either/or proposition. It's an *addition to,* not a *replacement of*, the readers' advisory services libraries already offer, including services that promote popular literature. In other words, I am not suggesting that libraries stop collecting or promoting popular literature. Such an extreme view would obviously violate our profession's code of ethics,[62] not to mention defeat the purpose of FVR, which again is foundational to one's development as a reader. Besides, as David Mikics points out, "Not all books are for all readers. You won't like everything, and you should not try—not even if the book in question is certifiably 'great.' "[63] The same goes for our users. But, Mikics also adds, we still ought to "stretch that taste, to see where it might lead."[64] We should encourage our users to do the same, that is, we should promote literary reading as a worthy challenge, as something that can and does bring pleasure. We should, in other words, add something else to our menu of offerings. After all, to make a choice, our users have to be given one. Promoting popular literature as if it were the only kind of pleasure reading is just as elitist as promoting literary fiction as if it were the only kind of reading that has intellectual value.

Notwithstanding these arguments, even if a librarian refuses to place judgment on *any* book, maintaining such a position still does not preclude him or her from promoting literary reading as pleasurable. And, as Evanston public librarians Karen Hansen and Lesley Williams point out in their chapter of this book, failing to promote the pleasures of literary reading may also be a disservice to our users. The first meeting of their yearlong book discussion on *Ulysses* drew 160 people! Clearly, such interest indicates that there are indeed readers who want to engage with challenging works of literature and who would like the support of a community to do so.

In building this community, libraries can best promote Slow Books. Conviviality—"taking pleasure in the processes of cooking, eating, and sharing meals with others"[65]—is central to the slow food movement, and it is a concept from which Slow Books also borrows. In fact, one of the reasons that books may currently lack appeal is because of their solitary image. At least digital technologies, through social media platforms, offer the semblance of companionship. But more often than not, books are associated with solitude. There is some truth to this connotation. For example, in the early 1990s, literacy researcher Deborah Keller-Cohen observed that many images of reading (on posters, bookmarks, book bags, etc.), including those of ALA reading campaigns, depict individuals in solitary reading acts.[66] Although it is usually the case that when we read, we read alone, such depictions obscure the fact that reading also helps us connect with others—to the author, to other worlds and cultures, and to other readers. In other words, books have the power to "bind communities together."[67] The chapters in this book will describe specific ways that libraries have achieved this community.

Slow Books at *Every Stage*

Although school libraries have long supported children's literacy—and public libraries excel at providing readers' advisory services for readers of all ages—one population eludes their grasp: college-aged young adults. This, again, is the same population that the NEA found to be among the least read (second only to adults aged 65 years or older). Although there is no single cause for this situation, it certainly does not help that the number of public schools with full-time library media specialists has been declining for the past several years,[68] and not all of these students have had easy access to a public library. From these data, it is reasonable to conclude that many students will arrive at college having never had a readers' advisory experience.

Perhaps, too, college is the reason that so many young adults are not reading for pleasure. Focused on studying and socializing, students do not have a lot of time for pleasure reading. Nonetheless, the fact that college-aged students are the least read might be one indication that academic libraries ought to be more deliberate in creating a culture of reading on their campuses. By promoting recreational reading, academic libraries recognize reading as a value and convey to students that forming a reading habit is also a part of their education. In addition, by teaching students how to follow the path of their own curiosity (e.g., by giving students the skills they need to identify their reading preferences and locate desired reading), libraries can also accomplish their information literacy objectives, as these skills enable lifelong learning.

Although the Slow Books movement is not unique to academic libraries, this book gives them special attention simply because (1) their constituents are among the least read in America; (2) academic libraries have tended to ignore the individual reading needs of college-aged readers; and (3) promoting recreational reading in academic libraries builds continuity between school and public library services so that library use is encouraged during and *after* college, that is, throughout one's lifetime. Still, this book is also for school and public librarians who are—of course—tasked with nurturing literacy skills. Although I think there is something to glean from each chapter, Part III of this book will be especially relevant to them, as it presents ways that school, public, and academic librarians can work together to address gaps in literacy skills and promote lifetime library use.

NOTES

1. National Endowment for the Arts, *Reading at Risk: A Survey of Literary Reading in America* (Washington, DC: National Endowment for the Arts), 3, accessed September 10, 2013, http://www.nea.gov/pub/readingatrisk.pdf.
2. Ibid.
3. Ibid., 9.
4. National Endowment for the Arts, *To Read or Not to Read: A Question of National Consequence* (Washington, DC: National Endowment for the Arts), 5, accessed September 10, 2013, http://www.nea.gov/research/toread.pdf.
5. David Mikics, *Slow Reading in a Hurried Age* (Cambridge, MA: Belknap, 2013), 7.
6. Kristin Purcell et al., *How Teens Do Research in the Digital World* (Washington, DC: Pew Research Center's Internet & American Life Project, 2012), 2, accessed January 21, 2014, http://www.pewinternet.org/~/media//Files/Reports/2012/PIP_TeacherSurvey ReportWithMethodology110112.pdf
7. Sven Birkerts, *The Gutenberg Elegies: The Fate of Reading in the Electronic Age* (Boston: Faber and Faber, 1994), 20.
8. Ibid.
9. Jonathan Franzen, "The Reader in Exile," in *How to be Alone: Essays* (New York: Farrar, Straus, and Giroux/Picador, 2003), 178.
10. David Mickics, *Slow Reading in a Hurried Age*, 18.
11. Ladette Randolph, "Introduction," 8.
12. Mickics, *Slow Reading in a Hurried Age*, 18.
13. Nicholas Carr, "Is Google Making Us Stupid?" *Atlantic Monthly*, July/August 2008, 57.
14. Ibid.
15. Marshall McLuhan and Lewis H. Lapham, *Understanding Media: The Extensions of Man* (Cambridge, MA: MIT Press, 1994), 7.
16. Maryanne Wolf, *Proust and the Squid: The Story and Science of the Reading Brain* (New York: Harper Perennial, 2008), 3.
17. Maryanne Wolf and Mirit Barzillai, "Questions for a Reader," in *Stop What You're Doing and Read This* (London: Vintage, 2011), 171.
18. Wolf, *Proust and the Squid*, 14.
19. Ibid., 66.
20. Plato, *Phaedrus*, 275.
21. Walter J. Ong, *Orality and Literacy: The Technologizing of the Word* (London: Routledge, 2012), 79.
22. Nicholas Carr, *The Shallows: What the Internet Is Doing to Our Brains*, 122.
23. Ibid., 63.
24. Nicholas Carr, *Shallows*, 116.

25. Ibid., 120.

26. Ibid., 194.

27. Edward Tenner, "Searching for Dummies," *New York Times*, March 26, 2006.

28. Michael Merzenich, "Going Googly," *On the Brain* (blog), August 11, 2008, http://web.archive.org/web/20130203011354/http://merzenich.positscience.com/?p=177.

29. Nicholas Carr, *Shallows*, 77.

30. Ong, *Orality and Literacy*, 79.

31. Wolf, *Proust and the Squid*, 226.

32. "Information Literacy Competency Standards for Higher Education," ALA.org, last modified January 18, 2000, accessed February 28, 2014, http://www.ala.org/acrl/standards/informationliteracycompetency. It should be noted that the ACRL standards are currently under major revision.

33. *Public Speaking*, directed by Martin Scorsese (2010; Burbank, CA: Warner Home Video, 2011), DVD.

34. Commission on the Humanities and Social Sciences, *The Heart of the Matter* (Cambridge, MA: American Academy of Arts & Sciences, 2013), 18, accessed February 24, 2014, http://www.humanitiescommission.org/_pdf/hss_report.pdf.

35. For definitions of reading literacy, see Mark Kutner, Elizabeth Greenberg, and Justin Baer, *A First Look at the Literacy of America's Adults in the 21st* Century (Jessup, MD: U.S. Department of Education), 3, accessed September 23, 2013, http://nces.ed.gov/NAAL/PDF/2006470.PDF.

36. Commission on the Humanities and Social Sciences, *Heart of the Matter*, 10.

37. Maura Kelly, "A Slow-Books Manifesto," *Atlantic* (blog), March 26, 2012 (8:03 a.m.), http://www.theatlantic.com/entertainment/archive/2012/03/a-slow-books-manifesto/254884/.

38. Ibid.

39. Michael Pollan, *In Defense of Food* (New York: Penguin, 2008), 1.

40. Michael S. Rosenwald. "Serious Reading Takes a Hit from Online Scanning and Skimming, Researchers Say," *Washington* Post, April 6, 2014, http://www.washingtonpost.com/local/serious-reading-takes-a-hit-from-online-scanning-and-skimming-researchers-say/2014/04/06/088028d2-b5d2-11e3-b899-20667de76985_story.html. Similar to Kelly's article, in this piece, Rosenwald writes, "Word lovers and scientists have called for a 'slow reading' movement."

41. Miedema's term "slow reading" and Kelly's "Slow Books" refer essentially to the same concept. The terms are used interchangeably throughout this book.

42. John Miedema, *Slow Reading* (Duluth, MN: Litwin, 2008), 44.

43. Stephen Gandel. "Amazon's Knock-Off Problem (35 Shades of Grey, Anyone?)" *CNN Money* (blog), April 16, 2012 (6:58 a.m.), http://tech.fortune.cnn.com/2012/04/16/amazon-knock-off-bestsellers/.

44. Miedema, *Slow Reading*, 45.

45. Ibid., 26.

46. Ibid., 3.

47. Ibid., 26.

48. Kelly, "Slow-Books Manfiesto."

49. Carlo Petrini and Gigi Padovani, *Slow Food Revolution: A New Culture for Eating and Living* (New York: Rizzoli, 2006), 76.

50. Miedema, *Slow Reading*, 13.

51. Ibid., 16.

52. Stephen D. Krashen, *The Power of Reading* (Westport, CT: Libraries Unlimited, 2004), x.

53. Ibid.

54. Ibid.

55. Ibid.

56. Ibid., 1.

57. For a definition of literary fiction, see "Literary Fiction," Adult Reading Round Table, last modified September 2007, accessed February 24, 2014, http://www.arrtreads.org/bootcampliterary.html.

58. Maja Djikic, Keith Oatley, Sara Zoeterman, and Jordan B. Peterson, "On Being Moved by Art: How Reading Fiction Transforms the Self," *Creativity Research Journal* 21, no. 1 (2009): 24–29.

59. David Comer Kidd and Emanuele Castano, "Reading Literary Fiction Improves Theory of Mind," *Science* 342 (2013): 377–380.

60. Petrini, *Slow Food Revolution*, 7.

61. Ibid.

62. See "Library Bill of Rights," American Library Association, last modified January 23, 1996, accessed February 24, 2014, http://www.ala.org/advocacy/intfreedom/librarybill.

63. Mikics, *Slow Reading*, 39.

64. Ibid.

65. "History: A Delicious Revolution: How Grandma's Pasta Changed the World," Slow Food USA, accessed April 14, 2014, http://www.slowfoodusa.org/history.

66. Deborah Keller-Cohen. "Rethinking Literacy: Comparing Colonial and Contemporary America," *Anthropology & Education Quarterly* 24, no. 4 (1993): 296.

67. Ibid., 49.

68. National Center for Education Statistics, "Public Elementary and Secondary School Student Enrollment and Staff From the Common Core of Data," accessed September 23, 2013, http://nces.ed.gov/ccd/pub_snf_report.asp.

2

Slow Books in the Academic Library

Meagan Lacy

As an academic librarian, I was in the unique position of starting a Slow Books movement in an environment that is not especially concerned with students' pleasure reading needs. Because the missions of most academic libraries are to support student learning and faculty research, services that center on reference and instruction have naturally taken precedence. But as authors Rochelle Smith and Nancy Young argue in their article "Giving Pleasure Its Due: Collection Promotion and Readers' Advisory in Academic Libraries," "The argument could be made that fostering reading for pleasure is a crucial part of our mission, since it both supports those pedagogical aims and moves beyond them."[1] In other words, if the goal of information literacy is to form "a basis for lifelong learning,"[2] then graduates should possess the ability to analyze their reading preferences, create evaluative criteria based on them, and apply those criteria to select books that they would like to read. In other words, graduates should possess the skills they need to be their own readers' advisors. Librarians can empower them to do just that.

But first, students have to know their institution values pleasure reading and that outside reading is considered a part of their education, that it is a means of education. At a basic level, they need to know that (1) they can find pleasure reading in academic libraries (i.e., that such reading exists in the stacks) and (2) they can ask librarians for assistance in identifying and locating pleasure reading. For these reasons, academic libraries ought to fold readers' advisory services into their routine functions. They are essential in building a culture of reading on campus.

Coming to this conclusion, I started to introduce readers' advisory services at Indiana University–Purdue University Indianapolis, where, beginning in 2010, I held my first position as an academic librarian. First, along with a group of likeminded colleagues, I created a popular browsing room—a collection of *New York Times* bestsellers displayed attractively in a cozy furnished space. Then I took my Nancy Pearl *Book Lust* training and began booktalking in my freshman learning communities. I formed a book club. Initially, I thought these activities somewhat innovative—I certainly couldn't think of too many other libraries that were doing something similar. And consequently, I wondered why readers' advisory was not more routinely practiced in academic libraries. I combed the library literature for an answer and discovered that actually, it *had* been routine practice—almost 100 years ago! If pleasure-reading promotion had once been considered a role of academic libraries, when and why did this attitude change?

For answers, I continued to look to the past. According to Stahl and Hartman, the purpose of historical research in literacy is to "inform us about how our current curricular systems came into being and how to build a sound basis for future directions. It permits us to use past practices to evaluate emerging and current practices."[3] Readers' advisory is such "a past practice" that informs ways that we engage college-aged students in reading today. Tracing the history of readers' advisory in academic libraries reveals not only its value as a collaborative literacy practice but also its potential to transform student learning. In addition, by reimaging readers' advisory as a teaching method, libraries can further their missions to develop students into lifelong learners.

THE HISTORY OF READERS' ADVISORY IN ACADEMIC LIBRARIES

The history of readers' advisory in the United States stretches as far back as the nineteenth century, but it began to flourish in public libraries during the late 1920s. Jennie Flexner, the original readers' advisor of the New York Public Library (NYPL), is repeatedly cited as the leader of this movement.[4] She built the Readers' Advisory service at the New York Public Library in 1928—during the dawn of the Great Depression—and has written extensively on the subject.[5] Her lengthier works include the pamphlet *A Readers' Advisory Service*[6] and the book *Making Books Work: A Guide to the Use of Libraries.*[7]

In "Readers and Books," Flexner explains that the role of the readers' advisor is to help patrons identify their preferences and match those preferences with the right books. Through these conversations, she says, "There is time to discuss with all what their interests are, what they have done in school or college, and what they have read and so to help them determine the lines along which they want to continue their reading."[8] By identifying gaps in patrons' knowledge and formal education, Flexner's version of readers' advisory clearly had a prescriptive purpose. Titles were selected based on "their use for self-development"[9] and sequenced so that the reader could progress through increasingly complex content and ideas.

This is an important distinction to make when comparing readers' advisory services at public libraries to those at academic libraries during the same period. Academic libraries did not feel this obligation to instruct and guide students' intellectual and moral development. As Natalie Notkin explains in her article about the readers' advisory service at the University of Washington,

> In the public library this is presumably the only department where the librarian consistently recommends a book because it "would be good" for the reader. The question of pleasure derived from the reading is secondary. In the university the student continuously reads the books that are good for him in the spinach-like sense, and so the readers' adviser can abandon the utilitarian scale and choose the books for the sheer enjoyment they might furnish the reader. Thus, the chief concern of the readers' adviser becomes recreational reading.[10]

With its focus on recreational reading, readers' advisory in academic libraries during the 1930s more closely resembles readers' advisory in public libraries today than it did public libraries then. At the University of Washington (UW), readers' advisors created annotated author and subject files of all the books in the collection to help students find and select their reading. Each index-sized card in the subject file contained a few notes to help students evaluate the title. A document dated October 9, 1939, describes how annotations were written at UW: "The annotation should not be wordy, vague, or ambiguous. It should give the contents, scope, and point of view of the author, and when necessary, his authority."[11] Additional examples of outreach efforts at the UW and other academic institutions included book lists, book talks, articles in the student newspaper, displays, and lists of new acquisitions, which were sent to faculty and prominently displayed in the browsing room.

Browsing rooms, also called recreational reading rooms, began to appear in the early 1920s as well. A librarian at Smith College is credited as having conceived of the idea, and Smith was the first to establish such a space.[12] According to Guy Lyle, author of *College Publicity*, "The 'raison d'être' of the Recreational Reading Room is to provide a place for relaxation and the enjoyment of books for their own sake."[13] He mentions several notable examples in addition to Smith's: the Farnsworth Room at Harvard, the Deering Browsing Room at Northwestern, the Linonia and Brothers Library at Yale, and the Tower Room at Dartmouth. Some colleges and universities also experimented with dormitory libraries as a way of extending this service. A study of college residence halls for men at the University of Chicago showed that dormitory libraries were exceedingly successful in terms of encouraging reading.[14] It is important to mention that while most academic libraries at this time provided "open access" to library shelves, some did not. These browsing rooms were sometimes the only direct contact students had with library materials, a factor that might also account for their popularity.

In Lyle's *The Administration of the College Library,* a whole chapter is devoted to the "The Encouragement of Reading."[15] Unlike his previous work, he explicitly mentions readers' advisory and the need to employ a readers' advisor for the library. The fact that there were designated readers' advisors represents the starkest difference between recreational reading promotion in academic libraries during the 1930s and recreational reading promotion in academic libraries today. Minnie M. Hussey, readers' advisor at the Woman's College of the University of North Carolina—now UNC Greensboro—proclaimed in her 1936 article that the Woman's College was the first in the state to have a member of its library staff whose official title was "Readers' Adviser."[16] A 1939 survey of general reading programs in 83 small liberal arts colleges revealed only eight especially designated readers' advisors.[17] Although the title was exceptional even then, the fact that Lyle had advocated for such a role is in itself telling. Moreover, whether librarians were called readers' advisors or not, such a service was customary—routine—in academic libraries at this time. Today, such a job title would be unheard of in academic libraries. This is not to say that academic librarians do not offer some version of readers' advisory service—only that readers' advisory is not the priority that it once was. Compare this attitude to a statement made by John B. Kaiser, Director of the University Libraries at the University of Iowa, in 1927:

> Those engaged in education today view the Library not only as an "instrument of education," but as a "method of education" . . . The Library suggests to the student that he take time each week to read books on some subject entirely outside his regular work; that he make the acquaintance of some of the standard magazines never before encountered; that throughout his course in the university he learn to use books as tools and as sources of information; but that, above all, he learn to know books as friends and to experience the sheer joy of reading the inspiration that comes from intimate contact with the great minds of all ages.[18]

In this excerpt, Kaiser places explicit value on recreational reading, recognizing it as a pleasure, a part of one's formal education, and a condition of one's lifelong learning. Moreover, he assigns a definite role to academic libraries in fostering this habit—by educating students in the "method" of finding books and information to pursue their own interests. Although academic librarians continue to teach with this aim of empowering students to become self-directed learners, this attitude toward recreational reading is rarely felt today. Rather, academic librarians primarily focus on supporting students in their research and coursework.

Why did this attitude change? Some clues are revealed in the proceedings of the University of Wisconsin's Reading Guidance Institute held in 1965. Hosted by the University of Wisconsin's library school, the purpose of the institute was to resurrect readers' advisory services in both public and academic libraries. The fact that a conference was held for this explicit purpose suggests that the decline of readers' advisory was felt even then. An article describing the conference, entitled "*Return* of the Reader's Adviser [italics mine]," published in a 1965 issue of *Library Journal*, further underscores this fact.[19] According to Anne Edmonds, who delivered a paper at the institute called "Reading Guidance in College Libraries,"[20] readers' advisory in academic libraries began to fade with the publication of Harvie Branscomb's book *Teaching with Books*. In this book, Branscomb surveys American college libraries and reports on their educational effectiveness—the extent to which their efforts were integrated with those of the institution as a whole.[21] He concludes that academic librarians were dedicating too much effort to recreational reading activities and not enough to their traditional roles supporting student and faculty research. Specifically, Branscomb offers these criticisms:

> The multiplicity of worthwhile services which a college library can render has obscured in the minds of many librarians the primacy of this duty of aiding the work of instruction. While all librarians would agree that it is their duty to provide and circulate books needed in the courses of study, a good many of them are inclined to feel, if not maintain, that their responsibility along these lines ends with these activities. . . . Their educational task has been viewed rather along lines of general or recreational reading. . .[22]

In Branscomb's view, the principal objective of academic libraries is to support student research through reference assistance and instruction. While he may have been quite correct in his assessment that students needed more, and better, bibliographic instruction, his repeated emphasis on the role of academic librarians in supporting the "college curriculum" and "more serious interests" betrays his desire to elevate their status. This sentiment is felt in such derisive comments as, "The college librarian has a different task from his colleague at the public library."[23] He suggests that recreational reading promotion was a lesser task performed by public librarians, not academics, and in opposition to the educational mission of colleges and universities. In her presentation, even Edmonds advocates for a kind of readers' advisory that more closely resembles information literacy instruction than recreational reading promotion.

Edmonds goes on to explain that the period after World War II saw a "great boom"[24] in the building and renovation of college libraries and that these new spaces were designed to create environments in which students and books would be brought together. Undergraduate libraries appeared. The first, Harvard University's Lamont Library, opened in 1949. Reading rooms became commonplace. Closed stacks became open. Paradoxically, however, as books and students were brought closer together, recreational materials became *less* visible. Open stacks usually meant that both leisure reading and academic texts were shelved together. So, even though these materials were more accessible to students, they had no immediate way of identifying leisure reading from the library's other holdings—no way of knowing that the library had leisure reading at all. In addition, "Large reading tables gave way to individual carrels in recognition of the fact that reading and studying is a private and intimate affair."[25] Thus, as readers' advisory disappeared from the academic library so did spaces that lent themselves to more social, collaborative work. These new designs reinforced the concept of the library as a place for quiet, contemplative study and the concept of reading as an independent activity. This may help explain why, as Keller-Cohen observed, reading has become a less collaborative practice than in the past.[26]

READERS' ADVISORY IN ACADEMIC LIBRARIES TODAY

College libraries today focus primarily on supporting student and faculty research through their collections and through bibliographic, or information literacy, instruction. Information literacy is defined as "the set of skills needed to find, retrieve, analyze, and use information."[27] Such skills are essential in the Information Age, at a time when it is impossible for students to learn everything they will need to know about their disciplines during their four years of study. Since information is necessary to effectively solve problems and make decisions, information literacy skills are also essential to lifelong learning. For this reason, academic librarians either visit classrooms or teach credit-bearing courses that introduce information literacy concepts and show students how to do research. In this way, Branscomb's vision of the academic library has prevailed.

Although readers' advisors no longer exist in today's academic libraries, this work continues to some extent in most academic libraries. Displays and booklists are still common practice, and most academic libraries have a browsing room containing popular reading materials.[28] In the past 10 years, readers' advisory in academic libraries also seems to have received more direct attention in the library literature, and examples of more intentional outreach and promotional activities abound. The University of Dayton created a program called Porch Reads, which encouraged students in residence halls to read a common book.[29] At New Mexico State University–Las Cruces (NMSU), librarians led two reading outreach initiatives.[30] First, their annual event, El Día de los Niños/El Día de los Libros, connected local elementary school students, NMSU students, and NMSU faculty with Chicano and Chicana authors though storytelling and panel discussions. Second, they led The Big Read: Las Cruces. The Big Read is a program of the National Endowment for the Arts (NEA) that helps organizations develop community-wide reading programs and events—including author readings, panel discussions, and film screenings—that are tailored to a specific book (in this case, Rudolf Anaya's *Bless Me Ultima*). What distinguishes the NMSU programs from other reading outreach programs at academic libraries is the fact that they invited involvement from not only college students but also the community—expanding literacy sites beyond the classroom and more closely realizing Keller-Cohen's vision of literacy as a collaborative practice.[31]

Librarians at Virginia Commonwealth University also describe a variety of recreational reading promotion tools used at their libraries: (1) a blog, *Book reMarks,* that highlights the VCU Libraries' collections and reviews and recommends books, (2) a book swap in which books are left on a bookshelf to be freely exchanged, (3) physical and virtual displays that promote local literature-related events such as author readings and creative writing workshops, and (4) reading programs, including one specifically for incoming freshman similar to The Big Read.[32] In addition to many of these promotional strategies, librarians at Gustavus Adolphus College, a small private liberal arts college located in southern Minnesota, teach a partial-credit discussion course, in which students read a book in common as well as books of their own choosing and meet weekly for group discussions.[33] Barbara Fister describes this course, called Books and Culture, as well as another for-credit course, The Reading Workshop, in the second part of this book.

Clearly, readers' advisory is valued by at least some academic librarians. Nonetheless, as a service it continues to be the exception, not the rule. Barriers to recreational reading promotion include lack of staff and funding, a fear of creating the perception that the library is spending money on nonacademic pursuits (making it vulnerable to budget cuts), a lack of space for popular collections, and librarians' concern that promoting recreational reading will detract from their image as research and information specialists—creating the perception that they are like public librarians.[34] So, Branscomb's old fear lives. I want to argue, however, that promoting recreational reading is a part of the educational and instructional mission—not counter to it—and can be used, as John Kaiser originally suggested, as "a method of education"[35] to teach information literacy skills and therefore lifelong learning.

As Jennie Flexner complained of college graduates visiting the NYPL Readers' Adviser Office during the 1930s, "Why is the intelligent man or woman not able to follow his own defined interest from book to book? Should not education place in the hands of every reader, or potential reader, the means of selecting books about a definite subject?"[36] Nearly 100 years ago, Flexner recognized both the importance of recreational reading to one's lifelong learning and the need for academic librarians to train college students on how to identify and find recreational reading.[37] The time is long overdue for academic libraries to respond.

THE ROLE OF SLOW BOOKS IN HIGHER EDUCATION

Despite the fact that the promotion of pleasure reading and Slow Books is typically a low priority at academic libraries, the importance of pleasure reading and Slow Books cannot be denied. For one, philosophers since Aristotle have been making the argument that the literary arts further one's moral development—expanding one's ability to empathize and develop moral virtues such as compassion and tolerance. More recently, American philosopher and law professor Martha Nussbaum has argued that novels—by arousing powerful emotions and by inviting readers to place themselves in the characters' experience—develop a form of imaginative thinking and feeling about others that is essential for social life and, particularly, the administration of justice.[38] Limited empirical evidence further supports these arguments. For example, literary reading has been shown to increase self-reported empathy[39] and to enhance one's capacity to identify and understand others' subjective states.[40] These social capacities are essential in today's globalized environment. To flourish in it, students must develop these skills and abilities.

Readers are also shown to be more creative thinkers. For example, Kelly and Kneipp found that reading for pleasure significantly correlated with creativity among college students.[41] One implication of this research is that college students may benefit from reading assignments that relay factual information in fictional modes rather than through texts consisting only of information.[42] For example, a history professor might use Jane Austen's *Sense and Sensibility* to teach concepts about the Enlightenment and Romanticism. A geography professor might draw on Booth Tarkington's *The Magnificent Ambersons* to illustrate how the cultural landscape of Indianapolis has changed and developed since the Industrial Revolution.

Catherine Sheldrick Ross's research on pleasure reading as a source of information lends further support to this idea. Based on 194 open-ended interviews with committed readers, Ross identified several ways that pleasure reading has acted as a source of information for these readers by (1) awakening them to new perspectives; (2) providing models for identity; (3) providing reassurance, comfort, and strength; (4) bringing connection with others; (5) inspiring courage to make a change; (6) offering acceptance; and (7) expanding one's understanding of the world.[43]

In terms of college success, researchers have identified several relationships between students' academic achievement and time spent reading for recreation. In Gallik's study of the recreational reading habits of students, he found a positive correlation between "cumulative grade-point average and time spent reading for pleasure during vacations."[44] His findings suggest that the more time students spend reading for pleasure, the more likely they are to achieve academic success. He adds, "this relationship could indicate that students who spend more time reading have, in general, superior academic skills and . . . the ability for sustained attention and concentration necessary for academic success."[45]

Moreover, there is plenty of evidence to suggest that students are still reading for pleasure. They simply are not choosing the traditional texts identified in the NEA reports. As Salter and Brook point out in their article "Are We Becoming an Aliterate Society?" recreational reading is in competition with many other recreational activities: playing computer games, watching television, text messaging and instant messaging (IM), and talking on the phone.[46] However, just because students are not reading *books* for pleasure does not mean they are not *reading* for pleasure. Salter and Brook found that 79 percent of respondents searched the Internet for personal interest, and 85 percent like to email or IM.[47] By expanding the definition of reading to include these other mediums, a fuller picture of students' reading habits emerge. Curiously, from this survey, the researchers also found that students are more likely to read as a recreational activity when engaged in an academic setting—possibly because students are exposed to more recreational reading materials in this environment.[48]

Salter and Brooks's findings are echoed in Jolliffe and Harl's research on college students' reading habits as well.[49] Students in this study were first asked to complete a questionnaire about their reading abilities and their reading habits in high school and college. Then they maintained a reading journal, for two consecutive weeks, in which they noted details about everything they read. The data generated by these tasks suggests that students were actually extremely engaged in reading—just not with the reading that their classes required.[50] The texts that they interacted with the most were technologically based: email, instant messaging, and Facebook. At the very least, the fact that students are reading *anything* is encouraging. But, as was discussed in the previous chapter, digital media use does not encourage reflection and new thinking in the same way that book-length reading does. In this respect, the book is the superior technology. However, in the same study, Jollife and Harl note that reading experiences that were thoughtful and contemplative—as in book-length, "studious reading"—were relatively scarce.[51]

This scarcity is a problem. Again, one of the negative tendencies associated with digital media activities is multitasking, which fragments attention and makes concentration difficult. Katie Davis confirms this impression in her recent qualitative study of a college student's use of digital media.[52] The study shows how the student's digital media use, though it helped her to connect with geographically distant friends, seemed to limit her ability to form deeper friendships as well as to focus her attention on any one activity. Davis concludes,

> Although some teachers may feel unprepared to address their students' digital media use, regarding themselves as "digital paleoliths" beside their "digital native" students, this portrait highlights the need for and value of nurturing youth's reflective practices and providing them with spaces for sustained reflection and authentic connection.[53]

Since the purpose of Slow Books is precisely to encourage the pleasures of quiet contemplation and to provide those spaces for sustained reflection, Davis's conclusion stresses the need for and value of a Slow Books movement.

Librarians and other educators can draw upon these current pleasure-reading preferences—for Facebook, email, chat, and so on—to help students recognize themselves as readers, as people who *want* to read. In this way, we can build and expand upon students' existing reading habits rather than try to persuade or convince students that reading is a pleasure—which probably would not be very pleasurable at all! Then by helping students articulate what they like about their reading, we can help them identify criteria to use to select other kinds of pleasure reading. This, in essence, is teaching students how to be "multitextual."[54]

Despite some of these disheartening facts about book-length reading, it is nonetheless encouraging to know that students are engaged in reading and, furthermore, that they like to read. In Gilbert and Fister's survey of students' attitudes toward recreational reading, 93 percent of the 717 respondents reported that they enjoyed reading for leisure.[55] However, they also reported that they lacked time—spending less than two hours per week on leisure reading. Again, the researchers found that pleasure reading competed with other activities—namely homework and socializing with friends.[56] Nonetheless, the issue was *time*, not disinterest nor lack of access to reading materials.

So, *if* it is true that recreational reading is linked to academic success and lifelong learning, and *if* it is also true that students like to read recreationally but lack time, then an obvious solution would be to reward students for their reading. One possibility is to make recreational reading a part of the curriculum and literally give students credit. In Chapter 6, Fister suggests one such possibility. However, indirect means can also offer their own rewards. Promotional displays, common theme programs, and book club discussions could translate into the serendipitous discovery of a book, a means of connection with others, or a new insight. Such outreach strategies further advance the Slow Books movement by promoting a culture of reading on campus and communicating to students that recreational reading is valued by the institution and considered to be a part of their education and lifelong learning.

NOTES

1. Rochelle Smith and Nancy J. Young, "Giving Pleasure Its Due: Collection Promotion and Readers' Advisory in Academic Libraries," *Journal of Academic Librarianship* 34, no. 6 (2008): 521.

2. "Information Literacy Competency Standards for Higher Education," *ALA.org*, last modified January 18, 2000, accessed February 24, 2014, http://www.ala.org/acrl/standards/informationliteracycompetency. It should be noted that the ACRL Standards are currently under major revision.

3. Norman A. Stahl and Douglas K. Hartman, "Historical Research," in *Literary Research Methodologies*, ed. Nell K. Duke and Marla H. Mallette (New York: Guilford Press, 2011), 218.

4. For example, see Minnie M. Hussey, "Readers' Advisory in a Woman's College Library," *Library Journal* 61 (1936): 916; Helen Huguenor Lyman, "The Art of Reading Guidance," in *Reading Guidance and Bibliotherapy in Public, Hospital and Institution*

Libraries: A Selection of Papers Presented at a Series of Adult Services Institutes, 1965–1968, ed. Margaret E. Monroe (Madison: Library School of the University of Wisconsin, 1971), 19.

5. Jennie Flexner, "The Readers' Adviser," *Journal of Adult Education* 2 (1930): 76–80; "Tools for the Readers' Adviser," *Adult Education & the Library* 5 (1930): 3–11; "The Readers' Adviser Meets the College Graduate," *ALA Bulletin* 27 (1933): 18–22; "Books and Advice," *Journal of Adult Education* 6 (1934): 188–191; "Readers' Advisory Service: What Is It—What Is it Trying to Do?" *Bulletin of the New York Public Library* 41 (1937): 463–472; "Readers and Books," *Library Journal* 63 (1938): 55–56.

6. Jennie M. Flexner and Sigrid A. Edge, *A Readers' Advisory Service* (New York: American Association for Adult Education, 1934).

7. Jennie M. Flexner, *Making Books Work: A Guide to the Use of Libraries* (New York: Simon and Schuster, 1943).

8. Flexner, "Readers and Books," 55.

9. Ibid., 56.

10. Natalie B. Notkin, "They Can Read," *Library Journal* 63 (1938): 866.

11. Instructions on Readers' Advisory Service, October 9, 1939, Reader's Advisory Service, Box 2, 76-001, Circulation Division Records, University of Washington Libraries.

12. Guy R. Lyle, *College Publicity* (Boston: F.W. Faxon, 1935), 51.

13. Ibid., 52.

14. Leon Carnovsky, "The Dormitory Library: An Experiment in Stimulating Reading," *Library Quarterly* 3, no. 1 (1933), 65.

15. Guy R. Lyle, *The Administration of the College Library* (New York: H.W. Wilson, 1949): 227–251.

16. Hussey, "Readers' Advisory in a Woman's College Library," 916.

17. Lois Eleanor Engleman, "General Reading Programs of Liberal Arts Colleges" (master's thesis, Columbia University, 1939), 75.

18. University of Iowa, *The Hawkeye* (Iowa City: The Junior Class, University of Iowa, 1927), 44, accessed October 28, 2013, http://digital.lib.uiowa.edu/cdm/compoundobject/collection/yearbooks/id/21042/rec/8.

19. Eleanor T. Smith, "The Return of the Reader's Adviser," *Library Journal* 90 (1965): 3215–3216.

20. Anne C. Edmonds. "Reading Guidance in College Libraries," 1965, Mount Holyoke College Faculty and Staff Biographical Files, circa 1837–, Mounty Holyoke College (South Hadley, MA).

21. Harvie B. Branscomb, *Teaching with Books: A Study of College Libraries* (Chicago: Association of American Colleges, American Library Association, 1940), ix.

22. Ibid., 83.

23. Ibid., 84.

24. Edmonds, "Reading Guidance in College Libraries," 5.

25. Ibid.

26. Deborah Keller-Cohen, "Rethinking Literacy," *Anthropology and Education Quarterly* 24, no. 4 (1993): 301.

27. "Information Literacy Competency Standards for Higher Education," *ALA.org*, accessed February 26, 2014, http://www.ala.org/acrl/standards/informationliteracycompetency.

28. Julie Elliott, "Academic Libraries and Extracurricular Reading Promotion," *Reference & User Services Quarterly* 46, no. 3 (2007): 37.

29. Heidi Gauder, Joan Giglierano, and Christine H. Schramm, "Porch Reads: Encouraging Recreational Reading among College Students," *College & Undergraduate Libraries* 14, no. 2 (2004): 1–24.

30. Mardi Mahaffy, "In Support of Reading: Reading Outreach Programs at Academic Libraries," *Public Services Quarterly* 5, no. 3 (2009): 163–173.

31. Keller-Cohen, "Rethinking Literacy," 301.

32. Renée Bosman, John Glover, and Monique Prince, "Growing Adult Readers: Promoting Leisure Reading in Academic Libraries," *Urban Library Journal* 15, no. 1 (2008): 46–48, http://ojs.gc.cuny.edu/index.php/urbanlibrary/article/view/1268.

33. Julie Gilbert and Barbara Fister, "Reading Risk and Reality: College Students and Reading for Pleasure," *College & Research Libraries* 72, no. 5 (2011): 490, http://crl.acrl.org/content/72/5/474.full.pdf+html.

34. Elliott, "Academic Libraries and Extracurricular Reading Promotion," 39.

35. University of Iowa, *Hawkeye*, 44.

36. Flexner, "The Readers' Adviser Meets the College Graduate," 20.

37. Ibid., 21.

38. Martha C. Nussbaum, *Poetic Justice: The Literary Imagination and Public Life* (Boston: Beacon, 1995), Chapter 1.

39. See Raymond A. Mar et al., "Bookworms versus Nerds: Exposure to Fiction versus Nonfiction, Divergent Associations with Social Ability, and the Simulation of Fictional Social Worlds," *Journal of Research in Personality* 40 (2006): 694–712; Raymond A. Mar, Keith Oatley, and Jordan B. Peterson, "Exploring the Link between Reading Fiction and Empathy: Ruling Out Individual Differences and Examining Outcomes," *Communications: The European Journal of Communication Research* 34, no. 4 (2009): 407–428; P. Matthijs Bal and Martijn Veltkamp, "How Does Fiction Reading Influence Empathy? An Experimental Investigation on the Role of Emotional Transportation," PLoS One 8, no. 1: e55341.

40. David Comer Kidd and Emanuele Castano, "Reading Literary Fiction Improves Theory of Mind," *Science* 342 (2013): 377–380.

41. Kathryn E. Kelley and Lee B. Kneipp, "Reading for Pleasure and Creativity among College Students," *College Student Journal* 43, no. 4 (2009): 1137–1144.

42. Ibid., 1141.

43. Catherine Sheldrick Ross, "Finding without Seeking: What Readers Say about the Role of Pleasure Reading," in *Exploring the Contexts of Information Behaviour: Proceedings of the Second International Conference on Research in Information Needs*, eds. David K. Allen and Thomas D. Wilson (London: Taylor Graham, 1999), 343–355.

44. Jude D. Gallik, "Do They Read for Pleasure? Recreational Reading Habits of CollegeStudents," *Journal of Adolescent & Adult Literacy* 42, no. 6 (1999): 484.

45. Ibid., 488.

46. Anne Salter and Judith Brook, "Are We becoming an Aliterate Society? The Demand for Recreational Reading among Undergraduates at Two Universities," *College & Undergraduate Libraries* 14, no. 3 (2007), 34.

47. Ibid., 35.

48. Ibid., 36.

49. David Jolliffe and Allison Harl, "Texts of Our Institutional Lives: Studying the 'Reading Transition' from High School to College; What Are Our Students Reading and Why?" *College English* 70, no. 6 (2008): 599–617.

50. Ibid., 600.

51. Ibid., 611.

52. Katie Davis, "A Life in Bits and Bytes: A Portrait of a College Student and Her Life with Digital Media," *Teachers College Record* 113, no. 9 (2011): 1960–1982.

53. Ibid., 1980.

54. Maryanne Wolf, *Proust and the Squid: The Story and Science of the Reading Brain* (New York: Harper Perennial, 2008), 226.

55. Gilbert and Fister, "Reading Risk and Reality," 478.

56. Ibid., 482.

PART II

Promoting the Slow Books Movement in the Academic Library

3

Getting Started: The Collection, the Service, and the Promotion

Pauline Dewan

Students who discover that their campus library does not house extracurricular reading materials are puzzled and surprised. Academic libraries are typically far larger than the public and school libraries with which they are familiar. Why, they wonder, would these large libraries not collect good books to read? Over the past decade, there has been an increasing shift toward a more user-focused approach in academic libraries, an approach that takes into account the student perspective. Woodward points out that "those academic libraries that are prospering have been evolving deliberately and rapidly," partnering with their users and listening to their concerns.[1] A recent study concludes that college-aged students are far more interested in reading than librarians believe.[2] Many campus libraries are responding to this need and providing the books their students want.

As Lacy argues in the first part of this book, never before has it been more important to introduce students to the joys of reading. For the first time in history, a generation of youth has been raised on screen reading, an activity that is substantially different from book reading. In addition, numerous media distractions foster "continuous partial attention."[3] The cumulative effect of an "always-on" lifestyle driven by devices that ding, vibrate, ring, play music, or pop up on screen is both an erosion of attention span and decreased opportunity to think deeply and reflect.[4] Although distractions have always been a part of life, Wallis points out that "the mental habit of dividing one's attention into many small pieces" has reached "a kind of warp speed" in the past decade.[5] Slow Books is intended to counteract the negative influence of screen reading and a culture of distraction that makes it more difficult to read books in their entirety.

Leisure reading is instrumental in obtaining this goal. Research has shown that leisure reading makes students more articulate, develops higher order reasoning, promotes critical thinking, improves reading comprehension, and helps develop writing style.[6] Those who develop the habit of reading have a greater likelihood of success in both college and their careers. Reading a book from cover to cover is a skill, one that we assume students have acquired by the time they reach college. If they find it a hardship to read a book, they will not likely do so. Students who read effortlessly find reading a pleasure, but it takes time and practice to become skilled at it. As Ross points out, "Reading is an acquired skill. People learn to read by doing lots and lots of reading."[7] Reading for pleasure introduces students to book-length reading in a way that encourages it. Consequently, books—regardless of their content—have value for our users. Moreover, reader response theorists argue that all recreational reading, not just highbrow reading, is beneficial for users. They claim that readers enlarge "the meaning of the text by reading it within the context of their lives. Through their act of making sense of texts and applying them to their lives, readers creatively rewrite texts."[8] Consequently, any book can resonate with an individual reader and may spark a recreational reading habit that will eventually lead to improved reading proficiency and increased willingness to explore complex literary texts (i.e., Slow Books).

WHAT TO COLLECT AND WHERE TO HOUSE THE COLLECTION

To promote recreational reading in your academic library, consider creating a recreational reading collection. If you have no budget for leisure books, partner with your local public library, as Rebecca Malinowski discusses later in this book. You could invite them to create a display that would entice readers to visit their library and/or run a public library membership drive at the beginning of term. Another cost-saving idea is to use books that you already own. If your institution teaches literature or popular culture courses, you probably already have a number of books that students could read for pleasure. One problem with this option is that these books will be unavailable for leisure readers when needed for course work. Unless your institution teaches a large number of literature and popular culture courses, your collection may be fairly small. Depending on the type of courses, the books may be limited to a few genres. The Library of Congress classification system that most academic libraries use does not facilitate browsing fiction. Campus libraries, unlike their public library counterparts, toss the book jackets of their hardcover editions, a practice that further impedes browsing. Readers rely on book covers for plot summaries, author information, and book review snippets when choosing books. Ross found that avid readers made successful reading choices by using the clues provided by book packaging.[9]

Some libraries with tight budgets ask staff and patrons to bring in copies of books they no longer need. Readers can swap books or take them out on an honor system.[10] These books are not catalogued. Be prepared for your collection to dwindle if you choose this option; more people take such books than return or donate them. Another problem is that old paperback editions can quickly deteriorate, a situation that can discourage readers from selecting them. Another option for libraries with tight budgets is to rent books. Brodart's McNaughton Plan is an example of a service that some libraries find useful.[11] Because popular leisure books can go out of fashion quickly, it is easier to keep current by renting rather than buying. However, not all libraries find this option as cost effective as it appears.

Libraries that decide to buy new books specifically for a leisure reading collection can make if affordable by starting small. A number of campus libraries have started with as few as 50 or 100 books, adding to the collection as it catches on with readers. If you decide to buy new books for the collection, consider purchasing paperback editions. Their covers include essential author, plot, and review information. If you are able to buy more durable hardcovers, you can follow the lead of public libraries and protect the dust jackets with clear plastic overlays. Buying new books will create a visually interesting collection that will attract readers.

Whether using new, pre-existing, or borrowed books, you need to decide what type of material to collect. Aim for a wide variety of genres to suit a broad spectrum of reading tastes. Most campus libraries already own a number of literary novels, so you may want to supplement these with popular books. Whatever you collect, you should focus on books that users, not librarians, consider "great reads." Ideally, there should be a mix of both literary and popular works. Academic libraries collect fiction in genres such as the following:

- Literary
- Fantasy
- Romance
- Suspense/thriller
- Coming of age
- Crime
- Horror
- Graphic novels
- Humorous novels
- Espionage
- Historical
- Action/adventure
- Science fiction
- Mystery/detective

A number of libraries also collect current bestsellers and movie tie-ins.

Keep in mind that many students also choose nonfiction for recreational reading. Those who read nonfiction for pleasure do so for more than utilitarian reasons. Authors of interesting nonfiction books, like writers of fiction, "tell a good story, develop characters, set a scene, and create suspense."[12] Shearer reminds us, "Some works of fiction have remarkably little fiction in them and . . . some works of fact are shaped like imaginative works."[13] The following nonfiction categories are popular with readers:

- Biographies/autobiographies
- Exposés of social issues
- Survival stories
- True crimes
- Diaries/memoirs
- Contemporary issues
- Travelogues
- The occult

A number of these genres can be categorized as narrative nonfiction—"a style of nonfiction writing that adheres to the facts, but employs the literary techniques of fiction to tell a vibrant story about real events, phenomenon, people, and places."[14] No matter which genres you choose, it is important that you keep the collection current and deselect items with low circulation statistics.

The next major decision about the collection is its placement. Should the books be integrated with the rest of the collection or housed separately? Integrating leisure books with the main collection is a necessity when space is at a premium. Keep in mind, however, that books interspersed throughout the collection become invisible to students. Key to the success of an integrated collection is making the books noticeable through a prominent display of their titles on the library website. Whether separate or interfiled, the collection should have a link to the entire set of books, and this link should be easily located on the site. Librarians at California State University–Monterey Bay have addressed this problem by creating a browsable virtual collection of their print recreational materials.[15]

The majority of leisure reading collections in academic libraries are housed separately. If students are looking for a good book to read, they do not usually have a title, or even an author, in mind. A separate collection facilitates browsing, and research has shown that college students do indeed value "serendipitous browsing."[16] Books in a separate collection can be "quick" catalogued and arranged according to author. A color-coded sticker added to the spine of each book serves as a visual reminder of the location. If you decide to add existing books to a separately housed collection, staff could assign a temporary location code to the records, thereby saving the time and money involved in recataloguing items.

What is the best location for a separately housed collection? A place that is welcoming and includes room for seating is ideal. Library resources will be underutilized if students do not feel comfortable in the space itself.[17] Research demonstrates that "although some students may seek out the library as a place for interaction with the university community, others appear to be looking for a place to find relaxation and restoration."[18] A room or even a nook with comfortable chairs will attract readers and provide a spot to relax and unwind. If your library has an in-house coffee shop, a collection close to it will attract readers. Incorporating leisure books in an area for current newspapers and serials has worked well for many libraries. Spaces that are highly visible will promote the collection. If you do not have room for seating, consider placing books on shelves or racks in a high-traffic area that will call attention to the collection.[19]

USING READERS' ADVISORY TOOLS

Academic librarians who feel comfortable answering all types of information questions can be apprehensive about readers' advisory queries. Given the immense number of novels published every year, it is no easy feat to match readers with the leisure books they are looking for. Most readers know what they want but not how to find it. Typical readers' advisory questions are: "I have read all X's books; could you recommend a similar author?" or "I love fantasy books with strong women characters; is there an author or book you could suggest?" We know that we do not have to read all the informational material in the library to be skilled at reference queries. Likewise, we do not have to read all the recreational books in a collection to successfully answer readers' advisory questions. What we do need are the right tools to assist us. These tools can also empower our users once we point them out.

Readers often identify a genre that they prefer. ("I am looking for a detective novel.") Libraries Unlimited's Genreflecting books (e.g., *Fluent in Fantasy: The Next Generation* or *Perfectly Paranormal: A Guide to Adult and Teen Reading*)[20] and the American Library Association's Readers' Advisory series (e.g., *The Readers' Advisory Guide to Horror* or *The Readers' Advisory Guide to Street Literature*)[21] provide suggestions that are organized by genre and subgenre. *Make Mine a Mystery II: A Reader's Guide to Mystery and Detective Fiction*,[22] for example, classifies novels as amateur, public, and private detectives. Each of these categories is further subdivided so that readers who enjoy "lone wolf police detectives" or "lawyer detectives" can find lists of books that match their preferences. A particularly useful tool for academic libraries is *Genrefied Classics: A Guide to Reading Interests in Classic Literature*.[23] If your library plans to purchase only a few readers' advisory guides, consider the flagship book for each series: *Genreflecting: A Guide to Popular Reading Interest* and *The Readers' Guide to Genre Fiction*.[24] Each volume classifies books according to a wide variety of genres.

All of these guides also identify what readers' advisors call the "appeal factors" of specific genres and subgenres. Noted readers' advisory specialists Nancy Pearl and Joyce Saricks point out that readers are usually more interested in the particular "feel" of a book than its subject or genre. Appeal factors capture this feel, providing a vocabulary and formal structure for assisting leisure readers. As Nancy Pearl observes, "Appeal characteristics speak directly to why a person may like or dislike particular books. Because it is frequently not the subject of a novel that determines whether or not a reader enjoys the book, readers' advisory tools that are purely subject-driven limit the possibility that readers will discover some other book they will enjoy reading."[25] Listening for the vocabulary of appeal provides major clues to what a patron is looking for. Appeal factors such as an exotic setting, well-drawn characters, a nostalgic tone, an intricate plot, or richly detailed writing style can be the elements that readers are looking for in a book. Most novels are driven by one or two appeals. We can recognize these appeals by thinking about the strengths of a specific book, that is, those elements we would focus on if we were asked to describe it.

In *Readers' Advisory in the Public Library*, Joyce Saricks points out that although there are numerous appeal factors, the key ones are pacing, characterization, storyline, and frame.[26] Some readers, for example, prefer fast-paced novels while others enjoy books that unfold at a leisurely pace. Nancy Pearl identifies setting, story, character, and language as "doorways" into books; readers can enter a story through one of these four portals.[27] Her Now Read This set of books is organized according to these four appeal elements.

Libraries Unlimited's Read On series also classifies books according to appeal elements. These guides add mood to the traditional appeal characteristics. *Read On . . . Biography* and *Read On . . . History* can be especially useful in academic libraries.[28] Another readers' advisory tool of note, the U.K. website Whichbook, was created by readers' advisor advocate Rachel van Riel.[29] Users choose books by moving sliders to the preferred spot on a continuum (e.g., happy/sad, short/long, safe/disturbing). Readers make selections by using up to four sliders for each book.

Appeal elements in nonfiction expand upon those in fiction. In *The Readers' Advisory Guide to Non-Fiction*, Neal Wyatt identifies pacing, characterization, storyline, detail, learning/experiencing, language, setting, and tone as elements that are important to nonfiction readers.[30] For example, some readers prefer ample detail, others less so. Sarah Statz Cords's *The Real Story: A Guide to Nonfiction Reading Interests* is organized according to nonfiction genres and subgenres.[31] Readers who are interested in true adventure, for example, can find lists of books on subgenres such as survival and disaster stories, sports adventures, cons and card games, war stories, intrigue and espionage, and historical and exploration adventure. Within each genre, Statz also discusses specific appeal factors. The problem with all these print resources, however, is that they eventually become dated.

Libraries that can afford only a couple of key tools should consider three excellent databases: What Do I Read Next, NoveList, and NoveList Plus. What Do I Read Next provides brief synopsis of books (both fiction and nonfiction) and is searchable in a variety of ways: genre, character, topic, setting, and time period. Users can also type in a title of a book they have enjoyed and find a "read-alike." NoveList Plus, which offers the same features as NoveList but includes nonfiction, is another useful tool. If libraries own only one readers' advisory database, it is usually this one. Like What Do I Read Next, NoveList Plus provides summaries of books and is searchable by genre, subject, and keyword. Users can search for a personalized combination of preferred elements (for example, vampires and exotic settings) and find a list of books that match their preferences. When readers click on the title of a book, they find a blurb about the story as well as a list of appeal factors. All of these databases provide lists of read-alikes and award-winning books. Whatever tools your library owns, it is important to become familiar with them.

CONDUCTING THE READERS' ADVISORY INTERVIEW

Purchasing readers' advisory tools and being knowledgeable about how to use them are not enough. Librarians should also know how to conduct a readers' advisory interview with those who ask for advice. The readers' advisory conversation is similar to the reference interview; the goal of both is to identify and meet the user's need. The first step is to make the user feel comfortable and at ease. As with the reference interview, librarians should appear friendly, approachable, and interruptible. Making the reader feel at ease is especially important in the readers' advisory interview since patrons have been taught that questions about pleasure reading are "less important than 'real' questions."[32] During the readers' advisory conversation, librarians must be nonjudgmental about reading preferences. Key to success is focusing on the user's preferences, not the librarian's. Just because you like a certain author is no reason the user should. Asking the reader to talk about a book she has enjoyed should elicit clues to preferences. Questions that are open ended will uncover hints about the type of book she enjoys. Starting with the question, " What are you in the mood to read today?" is another strategy that works.[33] Listen for the vocabulary of appeal—terms such as *densely written, unhurried, introspective, action oriented, thought provoking, heartwarming, suspenseful, poetic*. See Joyce Saricks's *Readers' Advisory in the Public Library* or NoveList Plus for a "vocabulary of appeal," that is, a list of words that identify these elements.[34]

Once you identify genre and appeal elements, use a readers' advisory tool to find suitable books. Some readers will want to browse the tools themselves. Encourage those who prefer to self-serve to do so by providing step-by-step instructions on how to use the tools. As with the reference interview, describing how to use the tool while you are helping them enables them to do so again later. For those who are not interested in the tools themselves, suggest rather than recommend books. Recommending books puts pressure on the reader to enjoy them. As Saricks points out, "Readers are far more comfortable returning with comments, especially negative comments, about books we have suggested than about those we have recommended."[35] End with a follow-up question tailored to the readers' advisory conversation. ("Do you have enough books to choose from, or would you like additional suggestions?")

Do not be intimidated by lack of familiarity with authors, books, and genres. Remind yourself that no one can possibly read everything. If you are asked a question about an author you do not know, rely on the tools, just as you would do with a reference question. However, to be skilled at readers' advisory, it is useful to be familiar with the specific appeal elements and characteristics of the major genres. A book such as Joyce Saricks's *The Readers' Advisory Guide to Genre Fiction* provides essential information on genres and their appeal characteristics.

PROMOTING LEISURE READING IN THE PHYSICAL LIBRARY

To create lifelong readers, we need to attract both existing and potential users. Even though the creation of a leisure reading collection can be the cornerstone of reading promotion, most academic libraries contain a vast array of interesting books outside of this small collection, books that could also inspire reading. Campus libraries, though, can appear dull, out of touch, and outdated. Consider how students may view your library in comparison with their favorite bookstore. Even nonreaders get excited about reading when they enter an attractive bookstore. Bookstore corporations carefully control the overall "bookstore experience." For too long, academic libraries have paid little attention to the "library experience." In her book *Creating the Customer-Driven Library: Building on the Bookstore Model*, Jeannette Woodward points out that successful big-box bookstores are little more than cheap warehouses, buildings that are transformed into attractive spaces by the clever display of books.[36] Academic libraries should consider modeling their approach on bookstores.

The other challenge that academic libraries face is the sheer volume of books. Hidden away in endless rows, these books become invisible to readers. The majority of books in academic libraries are simply collecting dust in the stacks. Many students enter libraries eager to find a book to enjoy. Faced with overwhelming choice, only our most persevering readers find what they want. If we can assist readers in making effective choices, they will be more likely to read. Ross found that appropriate reading choices became a self-reinforcing system while unsuccessful ones killed the desire to read.[37] Anything we can do to help students find the books they want and make the process of selection convenient for them will promote reading. Researchers point out that students do what is handy, and if reading material is not conveniently located on campus, they frequently choose another activity instead.[38] Indeed in a "universe of expanding choices among multiple media, attracting the attention of the reader is increasingly difficult"; readers must be motivated to select reading over numerous activities that compete for their attention.[39] In their 2011 study, Gilbert and Fister found that college students "would welcome efforts from libraries to help them discover reading material."[40]

Assisting students who come to the desk is a good first step, but this service benefits only the small portion of users who ask for help. Many others would read for pleasure if we made it easy and convenient for them to find what they want. Bookstores and public libraries know that readers need a manageable focus for selection. Book displays are promotional tools that academic libraries could use more effectively. Many campus foyers contain glass-covered displays of materials (usually rare books), but these displays have a static, "don't-touch-me" quality about them.[41] Such displays are not meant to circulate. By way of comparison, material in public library display units not only circulates but does so heavily—staff are continually restocking these units. The items in such displays are often ones that would have gone unnoticed in the collection. Public library staff also turn selected books on the shelves "face out" to highlight them.

The location of displays is as important as the displays themselves. High-traffic areas will attract users and promote themselves. No matter where else displays are located in the building, there should be at least one in the entrance area. Marketing experts know that first impressions are lasting ones. In fact, 80 percent of our impression of a new space is based on what we first see.[42] The foyers of many academic libraries are often curiously devoid of books and radiate an institutional feel that does nothing to entice readers. Book displays should be the first and last objects our students see when they enter and exit the building.

Themed displays are a natural fit for academic libraries and can be used to complement academic courses. Displays that include "both fiction and nonfiction bring together items from different parts of the collection. A display on crime could include true crime books, mystery novels, and works on criminology; one on World War I could contain historical books, biographies, survival stories, memoirs, and historical fiction."[43] We can borrow ideas from public libraries that have created popular displays on themes such as " 'a sense of place,' 'good books you may have missed,' 'journeys,' 'books for a long winter night,' 'open ticket: read your way around the world,' and 'books we're passionate about.' "[44]

Booklists are selection aids that allow for annotations—a feature that is particularly useful for browsers and potential readers. Reading maps, a variation on booklists, are web-based visual counterparts that encourage readers to follow threads of interest sparked by a book. Based on the idea of concept mapping, a reading map can link to websites, reviews, similar books, podcasts, interviews, and a variety of media. These maps are a visual and holistic way of promoting the collection.[45] Spicynodes is an example of a website that academic librarians could use to create these maps.[46] Bookmarks are also convenient tools for readers and are less work than annotated lists. Bookmarks are particularly useful for read-alike suggestions.

Creating a culture of reading in your library can begin with an imaginative poster campaign. "Clever advertisers promote their products and services," observe Van Riel, Fowler, and Downes, "by helping consumers imagine themselves using them."[47] Providing our students with an attractive vision of the reading experience can encourage the activity. U.K. public librarians have done this by creating a series of successful promotional campaigns. For example, posters designed for their "Give me a break" promotion ask, "Do you fancy a short break, a long break, a surprise break?"[48] Posters depicting reading as an oasis from stress can be a powerful motivator for students. Also remember that a major goal of Slow Books is to educate users about the value of books in the Digital Age. An engaging promotional campaign can help facilitate this goal.

THE BENEFITS OF PROMOTING READING

We know that lifelong reading increases the likelihood of academic success. Research has shown that those who engage in pleasure reading attain higher levels of education and work in more financially rewarding jobs.[49] Books of all types have proven to be sources of meaning, wisdom, consolation, and inspiration for countless individuals. Case studies have shown that readers identify with parts of a book that speak to their immediate situation and skip over anything not personally meaningful or relevant.[50] And, again, avid readers report that books have transformed their lives by changing their perspective, providing a new model for living, helping them see life differently, offering an enlarged set of possibilities, providing motivation, giving inner strength, and instilling courage to make a change.[51] We gain new insight and a fresh perspective on our lives when we read about other times, places, characters, and ideas.

Although we can read books anywhere, we do not tend to do so in the midst of noise and bustle. We look for a quiet place set apart from the stress and hectic pace of life. Hence, Slow Books. For our students, the pace of academic life is accelerating, and the need to get away from it is essential. What the Red Queen observes in Lewis Carroll's century-old classic—"It takes all the running you can do, to keep in the same place. If you want to get somewhere else, you must run at least twice as fast as that!"[52]—seems even more fitting in today's hectically paced life. Reading facilitates slow living and the qualities of life associated with it—reflection, meaning, and authenticity.[53] "Our greatest desire," claims Taylor, "greater even than the desire for happiness, is that our lives mean something. This desire for meaning is the originating impulse of story."[54] And since stories create significant connections between separate elements, they are prototypes of meaning for our lives. If we can help students in their quest for personal meaning, we should give them every necessary support.

Promoting reading also benefits the library. As more college courses are taught wholly or in part online, and as the library offers more and more virtual instruction, etutorials, online reference assistance, and electronic resources, there are fewer reasons to visit the library building. In fact, as early as 2006, thirty-nine percent of college students reported using libraries less frequently as a result of Internet use.[55] Promoting reading and creating leisure reading collections can encourage students to view libraries as centers of engagement, relaxation, and reflection. By playing an essential readers' advisory role in the academic library, we can foster student success and psychological well-being while also revitalizing our institutions.

NOTES

1. Jeannette Woodward, *Creating the Customer-Driven Academic Library* (Chicago: American Library Association, 2009), 10.
2. Julie Gilbert and Barbara Fister, "Reading, Risk, and Reality: College Students and Reading for Pleasure," *College & Research Libraries* 72, no. 5 (2011): 474–495.
3. Duncan J. Watts et al., "The HBR: Breakthrough Ideas for 2007," *Harvard Business Review* 85, no. 2 (2007): 20–54.
4. Pauline Dewan, "Can I Have Your Attention? Implications of the Research on Distractions and Multitasking for Reference Librarians,"*Reference Librarian* 55, no. 2 (2014): 95–117.
5. Claudia Wallis, "The Multitasking Generation," *Time* 167, no. 13 (2006): 34–41.
6. Elliott, "Academic Libraries and Extracurricular Reading Promotion"; Barbara MacAdam, "Sustaining the Culture of the Book: The Role of Enrichment Reading and Critical Thinking in the Undergraduate Curriculum," *Library Trends* 44, no. 2 (1995): 237–264; Bette Rathe and Lisa Blankenship, "Recreational Reading Collections in Academic Libraries," *Collection Management* 30, no. 2 (2005): 73–85, doi:10.1300/J105v30n02; Cathy Collins Block and John N Mangieri, "Recreational Reading: 20 Years Later," *Reading Teacher* 55, no. 6 (2002): 572–580; Bernice E. Cullinan, "Independent Reading and School Achievement," *School Library Media Research* 3 (2000), http://www.ala.org/aasl/aaslpubsandjournals/slmrb/slmrcontents/volume32000/independent#effects; Stephen D. Krashen,*Power of Reading: Insights from the Research* (Westport, CT: Libraries Unlimited, 2004).
7. Catherine Sheldrick Ross, Lynne (E. F.) McKechnie, and Paulette Rothbauer, *Reading Matters: What the Research Reveals about Reading, Libraries, and Community* (Westport, CT: Libraries Unlimited, 2006), 45.
8. Catherine Sheldrick Ross, "Finding without Seeking: What Readers Say about the Role of Pleasure Reading as a Source of Information,"*Australasian Public Libraries and Information Services* 13, no. 2 (2000): 80.
9. Catherine Sheldrick Ross, "Making Choices: What Readers Say about Choosing Books to Read for Pleasure," *Acquisitions Librarian* 13, no. 25 (2001): 12.

10. One such lending library program is described in Renée Bosman, John Glover, and Monique Prince, "Growing Adult Readers: Promoting Leisure Reading in Academic Libraries." *Urban Library Journal* 15, no. 1 (2008): 46–48, http://ojs.gc.cuny.edu/index.php/urbanlibrary/article/view/1268.

11. Brodart, "McNaughton Subscriptions," n.d., http://www.brodartbooks.com/mcnaughton-library-subscription-services/adult/page.aspx?id=270.

12. Catherine Sheldrick Ross, "Reading Nonfiction for Pleasure," in *Nonfiction Readers' Advisory*, ed. Robert Burgin (Westport, CT: Libraries Unlimited, 2004), 118.

13. Kenneth D. Shearer, "The Appeal of Nonfiction: A Tale of Many Tastes," in *Nonfiction Readers' Advisory*, ed. Burgin, 71.

14. Abby Alpert, "Incorporating Nonfiction into Readers' Advisory Services," *Reference & User Services Quarterly* 46, no. 1 (2006): 25.

15. Sarah P. Dahlen and Steve G. Watkins, "A 'Novel' Approach to Recreational Reading: Creating a Virtual Collection on a Shoestring,"*Reference & User Services Quarterly* 53, no. 2 (2013): 94–99.

16. Karen Antell and Debra Engel. "Stimulating Space, Serendipitous Space: Library as Place in The Life of the Scholar," in *The Library as Place: History, Community, and Culture*, eds. John. E. Buschman and Gloria. J. Leckie (Westport, CT: Libraries Unlimited, 2007), 170.

17. Joseph C. Rizzo, "Finding Your Place in the Information Age Library," *New Library World* 103, no. 11/12 (2002): 457–466.

18. Lisa Waxman, Stephanie Clemons, Jim Banning, and David McKelfresh, "The Library as Place: Providing Students with Opportunities for Socialization, Relaxation, and Restoration," *New Library World* 108, no. 9/10 (2007): 430.

19. For further information on popular reading collections in academic libraries, see Pauline Dewan, "Why Your Academic Library Needs a Popular Reading Collection Now More Than Ever," *College & Undergraduate Libraries* 17, no. 1 (March 3, 2010): 44–64, doi:10.1080/10691310903584775.

20. Diana Tixier Herald and Bonnie Kunzel, *Fluent in Fantasy: The Next Generation* (Westport, CT: Libraries Unlimited, 2007); Nancy Milone Hill, *Perfectly Paranormal: A Guide to Adult and Teen Reading Interests* (Westport, CT: Libraries Unlimited, 2014). For the complete series, see ABC CLIO, Genreflecting Advisory Series, 2014, http://www.abc-clio.com/series.aspx?id=51789.

21. Becky Siegel Spatford, *The Readers' Advisory Guide to Horror* (Chicago: American Library Association, 2012); Vanessa Irvin Morris, *The Readers' Advisory Guide to Street Literature* (Chicago: American Library Association, 2012).

22. Gary Warren Niebuhr, *Make Mine a Mystery II: A Readers' Guide to Mystery and Detective Fiction* (Westport, CT: Libraries Unlimited, 2011).

23. Tina Frolund, *Genrefied Classics: A Guide to Reading Interests in Classic Literature* (Westport, CT: Libraries Unlimited, 2006).

24. Cynthia Orr and Diana Tixier Herald, eds., *Genreflecting: A Guide to Popular Reading Interests*, 7th ed. (Westport, CT: Libraries Unlimited, 2013); Joyce G. Saricks, *The Readers' Advisory Guide to Genre Fiction*, 2nd ed. (Chicago: American Library Association, 2009).

25. Nancy Pearl, "Introduction," in *Now Read This II: A Guide to Mainstream Fiction, 1990–2001* (Greenwood Village, CO: Libraries Unlimited, 2002), xi.

26. Joyce G. Saricks, *Readers' Advisory Service in the Public Library*, 3rd ed. (Chicago: American Library Association, 2005), chap. 3.

27. Nancy Pearl, "Introduction," in *Now Read This: A Guide to Mainstream Fiction, 1978–1998* (Greenwood Village, CO: Libraries Unlimited, 1999), xi-xvii.

28. Rick Roche, *Read On . . . Biography: Reading Lists for Every Taste* (Westport, CT: Libraries Unlimited, 2012); Tina Frolund, *Read On . . . History: Reading Lists for Every Taste* (Westport, CT: Libraries Unlimited, 2013). For the complete series, see ABC CLIO, Read On Series, http://www.abc-clio.com/series.aspx?id=51799.

29. Rachel van Riel, "Whichbook," n.d., http://www.openingthebook.com/whichbook/.

30. Neal Wyatt, *The Readers' Advisory Guide to Nonfiction* (Chicago: American Library Association, 2007).

31. Sarah Statz Cords, *The Real Story: A Guide to Nonfiction Reading Interests* (Westport, CT: Libraries Unlimited, 2006).

32. Saricks, *Readers' Advisory Service in the Public Library*, 91.

33. Catherine Sheldrick Ross and Mary K. Chelton, "Reader's Advisory: Matching Mood and Material," *Library Journal*, February 1, 2001, 52.

34. Saricks, *Readers' Advisory Service in the Public Library*, 66, NoveList Plus database.

35. Saricks, *Readers' Advisory Service*, 76.

36. Jeannette Woodward, *Creating the Customer-Driven Library: Building on the Bookstore Model* (Chicago: American Library, 2005), 223.

37. Catherine Sheldrick Ross, "Making Choices: What Readers Say about Choosing Books to Read for Pleasure," *Acquisitions Librarian* 13, no. 25 (2001): 12.

38. John O. Christensen, "Management of Popular Reading Collections," *Collection Management* 6, no. 3/4 (1984): 75–82; Elliott, "Academic Libraries and Extracurricular Reading Promotion."

39. Ross, "Making Choices," 8.

40. Gilbert and Fister, "Reading, Risk, and Reality," 475.

41. Rachel van Riel, Olive Fowler, and Anne Downes, *The Reader-Friendly Library Service* (Newcastle upon Tyne : Society of Chief Librarians, 2008), 20.

42. Ibid., 83.

43. Pauline Dewan, "Reading Matters in the Academic Library: Taking the Lead from Public Librarians," *Reference & User Services Quarterly* 52, no. 4 (2013): 314.

44. Lissa Staley, "Passive Readers' Advisory: Bookmarks, Booklists, and Displays," in *The Readers' Advisory Handbook*, ed. Jessica E. Moyer and Kaite Mediatore Stover (Chicago: American Library Association, 2010), 79; Saricks, *Readers' Advisory in the Public Library*, 140, 142; Van Riel, Fowler, and Downes, *Reader-Friendly Library Service,* 18, 21.

45. Elizabeth Coates, "Reading Maps: An Innovative Approach to Readers' Advisory," Reading Connections Conference, University of Toronto, September 23, 2011.

46. "Spicynodes," n.d., http://www.spicynodes.org/

47. Van Riel, Fowler, and Downes, *Reader-Friendly Library Service*, 10.

48. Ibid., 10–12.

49. National Endowment for the Arts, *To Read or Not to Read: A Question of National Consequence* (Washington, D.C.: National Endowment for the Arts, 2007), http://www.nea.gov/research/toread.pdf.

50. Catherine Sheldrick Ross, "Reader on Top: Public Libraries, Pleasure Reading, and Models of Reading," *Library Trends* 57, no. 4 (2009): 648.

51. Ross, "Finding without Seeking," 75–76.

52. Lewis Carroll, *Through the Looking Glass* in *Alice's Adventures in Wonderland and Through the Looking Glass* (1865; Middlesex, UK: Puffin Books, 1975), 216.

53. Carl Honoré, *In Praise of Slow: How a Worldwide Movement is Challenging the Cult of Speed* (Toronto, ON: Alfred A. Knopf, 2004).

54. Daniel Taylor, *The Healing Power of Stories: Creating Yourself through the Stories of Your Life* (New York: Doubleday, 1996), 1.

55. Cathy De Rosa et al., *College Students' Perceptions of Libraries and Information Resources*, 2006, 6-1, http://www.oclc.org/content/dam/oclc/reports/pdfs/studentperceptions.pdf.

4

The Library Book Club at Regent University

Harold Henkel

Where is the wisdom we have lost in knowledge?
Where is the knowledge we have lost in information?

—T.S. Eliot, Choruses from "The Rock," 1934

The Library Book Club at Regent University was born out of a conviction that reading great literature is not a hobby or pastime, but a prerequisite of self-knowledge and empathy. As Samuel Johnson put it, "Literature is a kind of intellectual light which, like the light of the sun, enables us to see what we do not like; but who would wish to escape unpleasing objects, by condemning himself to perpetual darkness?"[1] More than anything else, it was Johnson's view of the role of reading that convinced me that a core component of our mission at the library is to persuade the members of the Regent community to put away textbooks and journal articles for 30 minutes each day and read "Slow Books"—works that encourage self-examination, empathy for others, and the ability to think critically about one's worldview.

In a 1995 interview with the Canadian Broadcasting Corporation, the great literary critic Harold Bloom gave this apologia for reading the great works of the past, which really goes to the heart of the matter and is worth quoting in full:

> In the end, that is what the canon is about: the search for wisdom. One cares about wisdom, and one wants to be judged by wisdom. If one hasn't got it, one has to ask the biblical question, "Where wisdom shall be found?" And I suppose for me the answer is, wisdom is to be found in Shakespeare, provided you get at it in the right way. Wisdom is to be found in Cervantes, provided you get at it in the right way. That is what imaginative literature is for. It is for wisdom, it is for the highest mode of aesthetic experience, it is for cognition at the most profound level. Most of all, I think, it's for

> training memory, in the deep sense, because you can't think, you can't read, you can't write without memory. That's the function of the great canonical works; they teach you what is worth remembering and how to remember it.[2]

It is an irony of academic life that while the acquisition and creation of knowledge is at the heart of the university's mission, many students and faculty find that they lack the time to read for pleasure, let alone wisdom. In her study of British reading groups, Jenny Hartley notes, "Higher education can prove a poor environment for general reading groups."[3] An informal survey of the Regent Library Book Club in 2013 confirms that lack of time is the main factor that hinders participation in a book club discussion. And yet, if we accept Harold Bloom's view of the role of literature to "train" memory, an education without great literature is really no education at all.

Book club discussions offer additional "training" opportunities. For students, they can reinforce and enhance the learning that is taking place in the classroom. For faculty and staff, they provide opportunities for continued learning. Moreover, their sheer existence helps to build a culture of reading on campus and sends the message to students that self-directed pleasure reading is also a part of their education and is part of what it means to be *educated*.

Researchers are just beginning to study the physical, intellectual, and emotional consequences of heavy use of electronic and social media. A 2013 paper by Karla Klein Murdock, for example, finds a direct correlation between high use of text messaging by college students and sleep problems.[4] It is precisely because of the inordinate role that electronic, "fast" reading plays in our users' lives that it is more important than ever for academic libraries to regard teaching "what is worth remembering" to be a core component of their mission.

LITERACY AND ACADEMIC LIBRARY MISSION

In the first half of the twentieth century, academic librarians considered encouraging recreational reading to be a core element of their mission.[5] A perfect illustration of the symbiosis that could exist between librarianship and literacy can be seen in Edwin Osgood Grover, the library director at Rollins College, who in 1926 was named "Professor of Books." Grover taught a popular course in recreational reading and opened the first bookstore in Winter Park, Florida.[6] In 1924, John Boynton Kaiser, the director of libraries at University of Iowa, urged students to "learn to know books as friends [and to] experience the sheer joy of reading and the inspiration that comes from intimate contact with the great minds of all ages."[7]

Today, few academic libraries consider the promotion of literature and books to be a core part of their mission. While lack of funding and staff are the most frequently cited reasons for not promoting extracurricular reading, some library directors simply do not view this service as being part of the role of an academic library and even a potential threat to academic librarians' professional reputation as information specialists.[8] A growing number of librarians, however, have begun to push the pendulum back toward an earlier model of the campus library as an inviting place with books to be enjoyed: "We need to rethink our mission. Like public libraries, we can transform our libraries to be more community-, user-, and reader-friendly by resurrecting practices that have lain dormant for the past half century."[9] Sam Demas goes even further, calling on college and university libraries to "look to the *Mouseion* [of Alexandria] as one model for further integrating itself into the community it serves and for providing a unique cultural center that inspires, supports, and contextualizes its users' engagement with scholarship."[10] Book club discussions help realize this vision.

ADDING VALUE TO THE UNIVERSITY LIBRARY

In a 2011 report, the Association of College and Research Libraries (ACRL) argues that academic libraries need to "engage in the demonstration of library value, recognizing that the process is not one of *proving* value, but rather continually *increasing* value."[11] In an era of shrinking budgets and staff, it will not suffice for librarians who wish to promote reading on their campuses to point with pride to models from the past. They must demonstrate that professional time spent developing literature appreciation activities, such as a book club, will add value by contributing directly to the library's mission.

The ACRL's *Information Literacy Competency Standards for Higher Education* state that "developing lifelong learners is central to the mission of higher education institutions."[12] A 2007 report by the National Endowment for the Arts (NEA) found that between 1982 and 2002, the percentage of literary readers among college graduates fell 15 percentage points, from 82 percent to 67 percent.[13] Not surprisingly, this decline in literary reading was paralleled by a decrease in reading ability. According to the U.S. Department of Education, between 1992 and 2002, the percentage of bachelor's degree holders considered proficient in reading prose fell from 40 percent to 31 percent, and among graduate degree holders, the percentage fell from 51 percent to 41 percent.[14]

While *To Read or Not to Read* provides worrisome evidence about the decline of literary reading by the most educated sector of society, the academic library is "a natural setting in which to combat this trend."[15] A library book club has a special role in fostering a love of reading, because it is a *social* activity. According to Elizabeth Long, "the habit of reading is profoundly social . . . social isolation depresses readership, and social involvement encourages it. Most readers need the support of talk with other readers, the participation in a social milieu in which books are 'in the air.'"[16] In several places, the ACRL information literacy standards speak to the social dimension of information such as Standard 3.6: "The information literate student validates understanding and interpretation of the information through discourse with other individuals, subject-area experts, and/or practitioners."[17]

THE LIBRARY BOOK CLUB AT REGENT

A book should teach us to enjoy life, or to endure it.

—Samuel Johnson

The Library Book Club was founded to encourage reading the classics for pleasure. The seed for this project was planted when a doctoral student asked me to comment on an article he was preparing to submit for publication. The paper included a number of incorrectly understood lines from Shakespeare that had most probably been culled from a commercial quotations website. As tactfully as I could, I communicated to the students that the sections with the quotations would need either to be removed or rewritten, but the incident was evidence of something I had long suspected: Many of our graduate students have a very thin grounding in books that for centuries have served as a fundamental frame of reference for educated men and women. One of the ways that the Library Book Club contributes to the intellectual life and mission of the university is to encourage participation as a lifelong pursuit in what Robert Maynard Hutchins called the "Great Conversation."[18]

WHY CLASSICS?

It is a good rule after reading a new book, never to allow yourself another new one till you have read an old one in between.

—C. S. Lewis

We live in an egalitarian, multicultural age in which an attitude of exclusivity appears simply ridiculous. So the idea of a campus book club dedicated to reading "great books" will probably be viewed with skepticism by some librarians. Julie Elliott writes that not only was a mindset of elitism by some librarians responsible for the decline of the reader's advisory but that this former attitude may still be a factor in keeping some academic librarians from regarding the promotion of literacy as part of their jobs.[19] Martin Goldberg describes a number of academic library book clubs that have been successful by reading fiction and nonfiction that relate to contemporary issues important to the students, such as diversity.[20] So how does an academic library successfully develop a book club dedicated to the classics without incurring a charge of elitism or worse? At Regent, the answer has been to make literary quality plus diversity the main criteria for selecting titles and to be willing to stray outside out of our usual focus. To "wear one's learning lightly" is good advice (and good manners) for anyone in an academic community, and I like to think that the Regent Library Book Club can claim to wear its literary preferences lightly. So while our experience with works by Jane Austen (our number one author), Charlotte Brontë, and Charles Dickens have been among the best, both in number of participants and quality of conversation, a glance at our reading lists over the past six years shows that we read literally "all over the place."[21]

Librarians and other book club organizers who think they do not want to go anywhere near a distinction between literary and popular fiction may be interested in a study published in the October 2013 issue of *Science*. In the study, the researchers set out to determine if there was a quantifiable benefit to reading literary fiction as opposed to popular fiction, nonfiction, or nothing at all. In five experiments, the researchers found that participants who were given a passage of literary fiction (both canonical works and book-award winners) to read scored significantly higher in tests to identify the emotional state of people in photographs, a skill known as theory of mind (ToM).[22] Although more research in this area is needed, the study's authors contend that "Readers of literary fiction must draw on more flexible resources to infer the thoughts and feelings of characters. That is, they must engage in ToM processes. Contrary to literary fiction, popular fiction . . . tends to portray the world as internally consistent and predictable. Therefore, it may reaffirm readers' expectations and so not promote ToM."[23]

PRACTICAL MATTERS

In her study of book clubs in the United Kingdom, Jenny Hartley finds that "every group is different, has its own history, and finds its own way of doing things."[24] What follows is a summary of the operating procedures of the Library Book Club at Regent, as well as what we have and have not found to be successful.

The reading list for the coming academic year is determined during the summer by the book club coordinator in consultation with the library dean and faculty from the Department of Language & Literature. We read one book each month, although we are willing to spend two months on "must read" titles, such as Austen's *Emma* and Dickens's *Great Expectations*. Experience has shown that the number of members able to complete a book before the meeting begins drop at 200 pages, and that at 300 pages, less than half the readers will have had time to finish the book. Our informal formula for building a schedule is literary merit, diversity (in gender, country, and point of view), book length, and projected interest by the Regent community. While we do not solicit recommendations, we do give requests careful consideration and try to honor them if they fit in with the overall schedule for the year. In general, just over half of the schedule is made up of classics. Most of the remaining titles are notable works of the twentieth and twenty-first centuries, but there are exceptions: Last year, following the recommendation of a faculty member, we read *The Immortal Life of Henrietta Lacks*. Although in general nonfiction has not worked so well for us, this book, owing both to the subject matter and the strong opinions of the recommending faculty member (who agreed to moderate the discussion), produced a highly dynamic and provocative discussion.

Marketing for the book club and each title is done exclusively through electronic media. While we advertise on the university events calendar and listservs, our principal marketing focus is on the library's social media sites—blog, Facebook, and Google+ pages. I also design an attractive email each month that is sent to the members and anyone else who has inquired about the book club. All of our marketing emphasizes that everyone is welcome and that reading the book is not a condition of attendance. We actually have a professor of law and government who attends most of the discussions but tells us, "I don't read novels." (We are patiently endeavoring to convert him on this.)

Attendance is quite variable, but excluding special events such as the Big Read, we usually have anywhere between 5 and 14 readers. The most important variables that determine participation are the book and the moderator. Most of our readers are members of the faculty or staff. Participation by students is problematic, and some of our discussions have no student present. However, we have found that students do participate in significant numbers when we tie the discussion in with a university-wide event such as the Big Read or Global Roundtable. Another way of persuading students to participate is by inviting a popular professor to lead the discussion. Since book club events are published on the university events calendar, we also occasionally have members of the community present, including homeschoolers, retirees, and even faculty from area colleges.

As much as possible, we try to have a moderator with academic expertise in the book, such as a member of the university faculty. Not surprisingly, the more complex or rich the book, the greater is the need for a qualified guide. When I have asked faculty members if they will lead a book discussion, some have declined for lack of time, but most have been happy to share their knowledge and experience with members of the campus community who are reading purely for enjoyment and enrichment. Universities are places of hidden resources and treasures for anyone who cares to look. When the book club read *Things Fall Apart*, by Chinua Achebe, I asked a friend on the faculty who grew up in Nigeria if he had any interest in leading the discussion. He replied that not only would he be delighted, he had also known the author for more than 30 years. Before our discussion, the professor telephoned Achebe at his home in New York and spoke with him about his recent reflections on this seminal and classic work of African literature.

ADDING VALUE TO THE UNIVERSITY

One of the ways the book club has been successful over the years has been to look to for ways to integrate our reading schedule with the intellectual and cultural life of the university. The most important instance of this came in 2009, when the university library was the recipient of a NEA Big Read grant to organize a community read of Tolstoy's great novella, *The Death of Ivan Ilyich*. One of the NEA's requirements for the grant is that each partner must organize a book discussion of the chosen book. The book club handled the marketing for the discussion on campus and organized two discussions: one in English and one in Russian (we also supplied free copies of the text) for both native speakers and students of Russian.

Between 2009 and 2013, Regent University organized a Global Roundtable each February on a different region of the world. This series was established as part of the university's Quality Enhancement Plan (QEP) to increase the global competence of our students. Beginning in 2010, the book club's February book was selected to complement the roundtable and enhance students' understanding of the particular region of the world covered. So while the 2010 roundtable on the Middle East focused exclusively on the Arab counties of the region, our discussion of stories and essays by Amos Oz (led by a local rabbi from Israel) provided the participants with a perspective from Israel.

By integrating the reading schedule with the global roundtable each year, the book club has not only been able to enrich the events themselves, but since the QEP is an accreditation requirement of the Southern Association of Colleges & Schools (SACS), the book club's participation provided additional documentary evidence of Regent University's initiatives to increase students' global competence and understanding. Besides reading a book specifically intended to complement the Global Roundtable, we have tried over the years to support the QEP by "reading globally." To date, we have read works translated from French, Spanish, Russian, Arabic, Yiddish, and modern Hebrew, as well as English language works by authors from Afghanistan, Iran, Nigeria, Romania, and South Africa.

Another way the book club has worked to integrate with university events and to contribute to the cultural life of the university is to select works being performed by Regent Theatre and hold a discussion in the afternoon before the play's opening night. For example, for Regent Theatre's production of *Fiddler on the Roof*, the book club read the cycle of stories on which the musical was based—*Tevya the Dairyman*, by Sholem Aleichem—and invited a rabbi who speaks Yiddish to discuss *Tevya* and the world of Russian Jewry at the beginning of the twentieth century.

GOING ONLINE

From the book club's beginning, it had always been our goal to find a way for our distance students to participate. We tried to accomplish this by starting a group on the social networking application for book lovers, *LibraryThing*. Despite consistent marketing over several years, we never succeeded in persuading more than a few students to set up an account and participate in online posting. In October 2013, I created an informal survey that I sent out to all the book club members and advertised on the library's social media sites. Eighteen people took the survey. The most surprising finding was that 72 percent of survey takers indicated that they would either "quite likely" or "possibly" participate in a book club discussion online via Google Hangouts, Google's videoconferencing application launched in May 2013.

Google Hangouts is similar to Skype but allows up to 10 people to videoconference simultaneously for free (Skype allows only one). It also allows screen sharing and integrates well with YouTube, a useful feature, since we sometimes show a short clip of film adaptations of our books. After practicing with the software in September and October, the book club opened for business on Google Hangouts with the November and December discussions. Although we had only one student join us at each event, the connection was good, and the students clearly found the experience to be a meaningful way of joining our discussion. Especially when one considers that Google Hangouts is now barely a year old, I think that this is a very promising start and that we will in time be able to develop a regular online following.

FUTURE PLANS AND CONCLUSION

As Jenny Hartley discovered in her research, a university campus can be a difficult location for building a successful reading group.[25] Convincing students to take on more reading let alone discuss it are major challenges. Indeed, relatively few students have become regular participants of the Library Book Club, and it is in this way that the book club has not totally fulfilled its vision. Recently, however, we have had indications that building a reading group in which students participate in equal numbers with faculty and staff is not a futile effort.

At our discussion of *A Tale of Two Cities* in March 2014, three undergraduate students joined us—all first-time participants. When I asked them what motivated them to take on a longish and not exactly quick read at the approach of exam and project season, they all replied that they love Dickens and that the English professor leading the discussion had told them about it. This reply is revealing in two important respects:

1. Contrary to what is conventionally assumed, there are still undergraduate and graduate students willing, in the words of John Boynton Kaiser, to "learn to know books as friends" during their leisure time.
2. In spite of all our marketing efforts, many potential readers still do not know about the book club.

The fact that the library's marketing, focused on social media, is more extensive than it is effective was brought home to us by focus groups we held with on-campus and online undergraduate students, coincidentally also in

March 2014. The focus groups revealed a nearly astonishing lack of awareness of some of the resources the library provides, such as our own YouTube channel containing research and database tutorials. The students told us that the best way to communicate with them is not through library venues, such as our Facebook group, but through the newsletter emailed weekly to all undergraduates by the university. The realizations that (1) most of the library's marketing simply does not reach its intended audience and (2) we have students who find time for reading in their leisure hours suggests that more outreach to the faculty will help the Library Book Club succeed in becoming a reading group in which students participate on equal terms and numbers with faculty.

No doubt, some librarians may also view the emphasis by Regent's Book Club on the classics as another area we need to reconsider if we are to attract more students. While I think that greater emphasis on shorter classics, such as the novellas of Gogol or the shorts stories of Chekhov will be an effective strategy, it seems to me rather patronizing to assume that students will not read challenging literature in their leisure time. This view is belied by the three undergraduate students who found time to read and discuss *A Tale of Two Cities* with us. What is required—in my view—is not easier (or more "relevant") books, but more targeted and clever marketing. For example, next year, we will begin our second Austen cycle, reading one of her six major works each year over the next six years. In addition to working with English faculty in the college, we will develop nonthreatening and (hopefully) humorous messages to convince male students that Jane Austen is not a "girly" author but one who can teach them how "to be a man."[26]

In Diana Loevy's guide to successful book club events, the author admonishes that "there is no such thing as a perfect book club; each club is in a continual process of becoming the club it always wanted to be."[27] I cannot think of better advice for a reading group just getting started. In the end, it is experience and the memories of what type of books produce the most meaningful discussions that are a reading group's the best guide. At Regent, British classics and world literature have consistently resulted in the most participants and liveliest discussions. At the same time, in an academic community, it is important to keep an open mind and take advantage of an opportunity to do something new. We were initially skeptical about putting *The Immortal Life of Henrietta Lacks* on the schedule because works of history had not really succeeded for us in the past, and we had never tried a work of science. However, the professor's passion for the book's subject convinced us to take a chance on it. The resulting meeting was one of the most illuminating (and opinionated) discussions we have ever had and brought in several readers who had never attended a book club event. And that is perhaps the best argument for why every library should have a book club—to give its users a reason to read great books they never would have considered on their own and gain a new perspective on the world.

NOTES

1. Samuel Johnson, "A Dissertation on Authors," *The Universal Visiter and Monthly Memorialist*, April 1756, http://books.google.com/books?id=PiUJAAAAQAAJ&dq=%22Literature%20is%20a%20kind%20of%20intellectual%20light%22&pg=PA22#v=onepage&q=%22Literature%20is%20a%20kind%20of%20intellectual%20light%22&f=false (accessed February 14, 2014).

2. Harold Bloom, interview by Eleanor Wachtel, *Writers & Company* (CBC Books website), 1995, http://www.cbc.ca/writersandcompany/episode/2012/06/29/harold-bloom-interview-from-1995/ (accessed December 10, 2013).

3. Jenny Hartley, *The Reading Groups Book: 2002–2003 Edition* (Oxford: Oxford University Press, 2002), 35.

4. Karla Klein Murdock, "Texting while Stressed: Implications for Students' Burnout, Sleep, and Well-Being," *Psychology of Popular Media Culture* 12, no. 4 (2013): 207–221.

5. Janelle M. Zauha, "Recreational Reading in Academic Browsing Rooms: Resources for Readers' Advisory," *Collection Building* 12, no. 3/4 (1993): 57.

6. Julie Elliott, "Academic Libraries and Extracurricular Reading Promotion," *Reference & User Services Quarterly* 46, no. 3 (2007): 35.

7. "Library Day," *Daily Iowan*, December 13, 1924, accessed December 10, 2013. http://dailyiowan.lib.uiowa.edu/DI/1924/di1924-12-13.pdf.

8. Elliott, "Academic Libraries and Extracurricular Reading Promotion," 39.

9. Pauline Dewan, "Reading Matters in the Academic Library." *Reference & User Services Quarterly* 52, no. 4 (2013): 310.

10. Sam Demas, "From the Ashes of Alexandria: What's Happening in the College Library?" in *Library as Place: Rethinking Roles, Rethinking Space*, ed. Scott Bennett (Washington, D.C.: Council on Library and Information Resources, 2005), accessed December 10, 2013. http://www.clir.org/pubs/reports/pub129/demas.html.

11. ACRL Research, Planning and Review Committee, *Environmental Scan 2011*, report presented at the 2011 meeting of the Association of College and Research Libraries, Philadelphia, PA, 141.

12. Association of College and Research Libraries, *Information Literacy Competency Standards for Higher Education*, accessed December 10, 2013, http://www.ala.org/acrl/standards/informationliteracycompetency.

13. National Endowment for the Arts, *To Read or Not to Read, A Question of National Consequence* (Washington, D.C.: National Endowment for the Arts, 2007), accessed December 10, 2013, http://arts.gov/sites/default/files/ToRead.pdf, 8.

14. Ibid, 12.

15. Renée Bosman, John Glover, and Monique Prince, "Growing Adult Readers: Promoting Reading in Academic Libraries," *Urban Library Journal* 15, no. 1 (2008): 46.

16. Elizabeth Long, *Book Clubs: Women and the Uses of Reading in Everyday Life* (Chicago: University of Chicago Press, 2003), 10.

17. Association of College and Research Libraries, *Information Literacy Competency Standards for Higher Education.*

18. Britannica Editors, " 'The Great Conversation' (The Classic Essay for the Great Books by Robert Hutchins)," *Encyclopaedia Britannica Blog*, December 11, 2008, accessed February 14, 2014, http://www.britannica.com/blogs/2008/12/the-great-conversation-robert-hutchinss-essay-for-the-great-books/.

19. Elliott, "Academic Libraries and Extracurricular Reading Promotion," 36.

20. Martin Goldberg, "Extracurricular Reading: Creating and Sustaining On Campus Book Clubs," *Reference & User Services Quarterly* 51, no. 3 (2012): 231–234.

21. Regent University Library, "Library Book Club," accessed December 10, 2013, http://libguides.regent.edu/bookclub?hs=a.

22. *Encyclopedia of Consciousness,* s.v., "Theory **of** Mind (Neural Basis)" (Oxford: Elsevier Science & Technology, 2009), accessed December 10, 2013, http://www.sciencedirect.com/science/article/pii/B9780123738738000785.

23. David Comer Kidd and Emanuele Castano, "Reading Literary Fiction Improves Theory of Mind," *Science* 342, no. 6156 (2013): 378.

24. Hartley, *Reading Groups Book,* xii.

25. Hartley, *Reading Groups Book,* 35.

26. Deresiewicz William, "How Jane Austen Taught Me to Be a Man," *Wall Street Journal, Eastern Edition*, May 13, 2011, http://online.wsj.com/news/articles/SB10001424052748704004004576270762735324994.

27. Diana Loevy, *The Book Club Companion: A Comprehensive Guide to the Reading Group Experience* (New York: Berkley, 2006), 1.

5

TEN YEARS OF THEME READING AT INDIANA UNIVERSITY SOUTH BEND

Julie Elliott

"One Book" community reading programs began only a little over a decade ago, in 1998, when Nancy Pearl, then the executive director for the Washington Center for the Book at the Seattle Public Library, initiated her program If All Seattle Read the Same Book.[1] The concept quickly gained popularity. During the 2004 ALA Midwinter meeting, ALA hosted a "One Book, One Community" workshop, the first training opportunity ever offered to "One Book Programmers."[2] And in 2006, in response to the dire findings presented in their 2004 report, *Reading at Risk*, the National Endowment for the Arts inaugurated the Big Read as a pilot project. Now in its eighth year, the Big Read supports organizations across the United States in developing community-wide reading programs. Organizations selected to participate in the Big Read "receive a grant, access to online training resources and opportunities, and promotional materials designed to support widespread community involvement."[3] Several academic libraries have since participated in the Big Read or have created their own One Book programs.[4] The strength of this program is the way that it builds community through reading. By reading and discussing a single work, participants connect to literature and to each other. Thus, One Book programs build and support a culture of reading—a major goal of the Slow Books movement.

The idea of a One Book, One Campus program at Indiana University South Bend grew out of the campus's revised general education program and the program's "campus theme." Through a campus nomination system, the library sponsored events and discussions on a book that was related to the theme year. The idea behind both the theme and the one book, one campus program was that every year, the general education courses would be created around a theme, and students would attend related events, thereby having a year-long discussion in a variety of courses about the same topic. The hope with the program is that it will help create a sense of campus community and foster a wider campus discussion of important issues. Although there are student leaders and engaged students at IU South Bend, and although important discussions take place on our campus, often students are talking only to those most like themselves, those who share a similar background and views. For example, a talk on Muslim life in the United States was attended by many of our Muslim students, but few other students attended.

The idea of a theme, as written in the original proposal is as follows:

> Classroom instruction is the appropriate format for most of general education. However, the university environment offers a multitude of other opportunities for intellectual and cultural growth—colloquia, film series, theatrical and musical productions—which with proper thought and planning could be used to further enhance the coherence and effectiveness of the general education curriculum. Toward this end, we recommend the identification of a theme—examples might be: The Environment; Revolutions; Science and Society; Africa; Ancient Civilizations—for each academic year, around which many of the year's co-curricular activities, as well as offerings in the *Common Core*, could be planned. This practice would significantly enhance the coherence of the general education curriculum, by providing an explicit and highly publicized example of a topic that can be approached from many disciplines. It could also become a highly visible and innovative signature feature of an IUSB education.[5]

The first campus theme, "Identity," was in place during the 2003–2004 school year. The library participated in the campus theme year with their spring speaker, author Cathy Bao Bean, who spoke about "identity by the chopstick fork principle." In the spring and summer of 2004, I approached our dean about doing some kind of common reading program similar to the One Book, One Community programs across the country. The first One Book, One Campus title was *War Is a Force That Gives Us Meaning,* by Chris Hedges. Through an Indiana Humanities Council grant and funds raised through working with the Office of Public Affairs and University Advancement, the library was able to bring in Hedges to speak. Expected outcomes of the project were (1) to increase participation in campus events by students and members of the Michiana community and increase consideration of humanities works by students and faculty members outside of the humanities (business, psychology, etc.) and (2) to provide students with the opportunity to apply their learning outside of the classroom (through events, discussions, performances, service learning activities, etc.). During the second year of One Book, One Campus (2005–2006), students, faculty, and staff suggested titles for the common book, which was then chosen through a campus vote. The winner was *Do Androids Dream of Electric Sheep*? by Philip K. Dick, which complemented the campus theme, the "Mutable Body." Several faculty incorporated the theme and book into their courses.

We have since had eight more One Book, One Campus programs. These programs have both raised the library's profile on campus and connected students, faculty, and staff through discussion of a common work. That said, One Book, One Campus programs can be time consuming and require patience and diplomacy. Successful themes also need to be carefully planned and receive full campus support to be truly successful. Major suggestions for anyone thinking of starting a One Book, One Campus theme program are to integrate the theme with course offerings, tie your programming to specific goals, create assessments, and collect data.

COURSE INTEGRATION

During the first couple of years of the One Book, Campus Theme partnership, I would try a little bit of everything. Book discussions led by students, faculty, and myself were held both on and off campus. These were mainly unsuccessful (discussion was always interesting, but with the exception of two discussions related to the first book—*War is a Force That Gives Us Meaning*—that were attended by members of the local Peace and Justice Coalition, the attendance numbers were very, very low). A blog was created, and postings from students were encouraged (this worked best with the science fiction classic *Do Androids Dream of Electric Sheep*?), but I wrote most of the postings. In discussion with faculty while promoting the various one book speaker events, I discovered that many of the students attending these activities were reading the book in a course—from what I could determine, students and faculty were not reading the book on their own time. So, beginning with the third title, *The Spirit Catches You and You Fall Down*, by Anne Fadiman, we focused more on tying the works and speaker events to the classroom than we had originally intended and less to outside off-campus activities such as book discussions or the blog. Successful years featured works that could be integrated into a number of programs, such as:

2005: *Do Androids Dream of Electric Sheep?* by Philip K. Dick—adopted by courses within computer science as well as additional general education courses. Dr. Micheline Nilsen, an art history professor and coordinator of the campus theme in 2005–2006, received a New Perspectives grant to create a general education course on the theme the "Mutable Body." The course had many guest lecturers who spoke on the book and other related topics (the lecture portion of the course was also open to the public), and the course also discussed the film adaptation of the book, *Blade Runner*. The book was also taught in computer science, where students wrote essays for the One Book, One Campus blog.

2006: *The Spirit Catches You and You Fall Down,* by Anne Fadiman—adopted by many classes in our nursing program as well as additional general education courses. This work is still being used in some of our allied health courses. Two of our speakers, Dr. Neil Ernst and Dr. Peggy Philp (who were featured in the book), came to campus and spent the morning fielding questions from excited students who were enrolled in a joint history and English course titled Integration and Immigration.

2009: *There Are No Children Here,* by Alex Kotlowitz—adopted by the freshman U100 course and additional general education courses. Kotlowitz came to speak and also spent the morning working with various students in freshman U100 and English courses, answering their questions about the book. He also gave an interview for a podcast, which is available on our website: https://www.iusb.edu/campustheme/archives/0910/index.php

2010: *The Communist Manifesto,* by Karl Marx—a controversial title (and our only winning title nominated by a student) that presented some challenges (it was the first title without a "student-created readers' guide"). There were no funds to bring in an outside speaker for the work, so instead, I created a faculty-led speaker series that was well attended. The success of this event and the event the following year led me to re-examine our One Book events and goals.

2011: *The Post-American World*, by Fareed Zakaria. Zakaria's honorarium was way beyond anything we could afford, so, taking the success of the previous year's lecture series into consideration, we put together a panel presentation on the book featuring faculty in business and political science. I took suggestions from students about which faculty they would recommend for speakers and promoted the event as a chance for students to get a perspective on the work from charismatic professors that they may not have taken a class from yet. The event was very well attended and served in part as the template for the U100 partnership in 2012.

2012: *Nickel and Dimed,* by Barbara Ehrenreich—adopted by the freshman U100 course as well as several general education courses. Community leaders (including our mayor) and popular faculty came to briefly talk about issues in the book and then work with the students in breakout sessions, where the students led the discussions.

GOALS

The original goal of the One Book program at IU South Bend was to encourage critical thinking among students, faculty, and staff through the discussion of one book. Several years in, we found this goal was too broad.

In consultation with the freshman course, we began collaborating as our goals became more specific to reflect the university's increased focus on retention. The goals are as follows: (1) to introduce students to reading, critical thinking, and the kinds of discussions they will experience at Indiana University South Bend; (2) to create a sense of campus community through shared student and faculty interaction with a work; and (3) to provide an opportunity for students to take material learned in the classroom and apply it to out of class experiences (in the form of events, performances, service learning activities, etc.). We have since revised our programming to meet these goals. For example, in 2012, for *Nickel and Dimed*, we held a morning-long program that focused more on students interacting with the speakers than the more passive structure of a speaker lecture. We plan to continue to review our goals every three to five years to re-evaluate and revise them as necessary.

PROGRAMMING

While our primary audience has been the students, faculty, and staff of IU South Bend, we have experimented with off-campus book discussions (at Borders as well as at Barnes & Noble). Our speaker events are free and open to the public and have been promoted in the past throughout the Michiana community through WVPE radio ads as well as in ads and press releases sent to the *South Bend Tribune*. Our audience is mainly students and faculty at IU South Bend, but we do have community participation. In the spring of 2014, we experimented with bringing a speaker to talk at a local middle school as well as a community event off campus, and we are currently assessing how well this community outreach works.

Even during off years for course integration, such as 2011, One Book, One Campus has always had strong event programming to support it. Programming highlights include a *Communist Manifesto* speaker series by faculty from the history department, a presentation from the doctors in *The Spirit Catches You and You Fall Down*, Alex Kotlowitz's day-long visit, and a theatre production of *Paragon Springs*, an adaptation of 2007's One Book title, *An Enemy of the People*.

Promotion of the events works best through word of mouth advertising. I begin promoting book as soon as possible to professors, sending reminders at the end of each semester as they were working on finalizing their syllabi for the next semester.

IS BRINGING THE AUTHOR WORTH IT?

Big name speakers are not always worth the cost and effort. For every visit during which the speaker is willing to meet with classes and be interviewed for podcasts (such as Alex Kotlowitz) there are speakers to whom you end up paying thousands of dollars to merely read a chapter of their book out loud.

After experiencing this disappointment once, we had to rethink what goals we wanted our events to meet. We found that bringing in speakers who are willing to talk to a class or group of classes, in addition to an evening lecture, is extremely important.

But even when we were unable to bring in the author (say, if the author was dead, unavailable, or just too expensive), we've found that using area experts or our own faculty is just as effective, especially if readers connect with the book. These events could be funded through a few key departments chipping in funds. These departments also serve as great advocates for drawing people to the events. We found that this kind of local programming tied well with classes, exposing students to additional perspectives, not just those of their professors. These events also serve as a way for students to preview professors they have not yet taken a course from.

Whether you invite the author or your own faculty, capitalize on any successful program. Always have a program evaluation sheet and quickly analyze the information you get from it. Take a lot of photographs and keep them where they can be easily found and shared. Do a write-up with faculty and student quotes for campus publications. Do a short write-up with a faculty slant and send it to faculty and key administrators. If you do not publicize widely now, people will forget later.

ISSUES AND CONCERNS TO ADDRESS IMMEDIATELY

One thing I've learned is that you have to identify what is not working and respond. One feature of our program was a vote—books were nominated by students, faculty, and staff and then voted on. Despite our best efforts, only a small fraction of the campus took part in the vote. While the vote was a nice idea that led to some fun works over the years, it also led to some titles that left faculty and students cold. After a couple of years of less than successful programs, I regrouped and reevaluated and determined—again—that the One Book program works best when it is tied to a course. With that in mind, I approached the coordinator of the freshman U100 course about a partnership, she agreed, and we put together a team of U100 instructors to create the 2012 One Book event. Faculty have informed me that they like having their students consider information from the faculty presentations and work them into their research papers. With this feedback, we concluded that instead of trying to pitch to new courses every year, we would tie the book to one major course from the start and allow the course faculty to select the book.

We are now working with a freshman course (U100) with a built-in audience of 450, and we're focusing on low-cost events featuring our faculty and local community leaders. This strategy saves us from fundraising issues and has allowed us to refine our goals in ways that can be more easily assessed. Other considerations to be mindful of are:

Theme selection. The general education task force in 2003 recommended that the theme be announced "at least a year in advance of the beginning of its effective academic year."[6] They noted that they should choose the first theme, and possibly the second, since the general education curriculum would not yet be fully in effect. There is no mention in the report of how subsequent themes would be chosen. This became a problem at IU South Bend.

Leadership. It must be clear how the theme will be chosen, how theme leaders will be compensated, and what the expectations for their performance are. Finding people who are willing to coordinate a theme for a year was difficult. It was also more difficult because it was unclear whether the coordinators would get any release time for their efforts, which can be a factor in whether one is willing to do this.

Budget. There should be one. Because there has never been a budget for One Book, One Campus, every year, I have to look to others to help fund whatever speakers we want to invite. Because the theme year's funding varies from year to year, it is hard to plan a consistent program that meets campus expectations. As part of the partnership with the freshman course, in the spring of 2014, we applied for, and received, a campus grant that will allow us to continue to fund the project. Finding a consistent, long-term funding source for your project is very important.

RECOMMENDED TIMELINE FOR THEME AND ONE BOOK PLANNING

As most university courses are created and added to the academic calendar well over a year ahead of time, themes and books should be chosen two years out to give time for classes to be created. For example:

2014–2015: chosen by start of fall semester 2012
2015–2016: chosen by start of fall semester 2013
2016–2017: chosen by start of fall semester 2014

ASSESSMENT DATA, OR ADMINISTRATORS CHANGE, BE READY

When you work on a long-running program, you need to be prepared for a change in administration. The administrators who supported your project may retire or move on, and new administrators may be interested in trying new things. If you want to keep your project going, it will help if you have assessment data ready to share. For Common Theme and One Book programs, project coordinators should write annual reports that detail the number of courses that include the theme and the number of courses that include the book. Event assessment is useful, but if the event is tied to course participation, assessment data that shares whether the event helped the students' understanding of theme issues demonstrates actual impact (rather than just information on attendance or participant satisfaction). I had to develop this kind of student-centered assessment data eight years into the One Book program (I had always had program assessment data), and I am still revising it. I highly recommend that anyone beginning such a program create their student-centered assessment measurements immediately. Questions to be considered in student-centered assessment should include whether students found the work helped them understand their coursework better and whether it helped them feel more connected to the campus.

If you are several years into a program and have not yet created student-centered assessment, even compiling whatever kind of assessment data you have is useful. I had eight years of strong numbers for event attendance, and this data did help convince administrators on my campus to continue the program during a down year. Also keep in mind that assessment data is valuable not only to administrators. My list of program compliments from faculty whose students enjoyed the program helped convince new collaborators to work with me on the program. For this reason, you should keep a file of any positive feedback you receive from students and faculty. Circulation statistics are also useful for making our case to library colleagues, especially if theme year and One Book titles continue to circulate well after the theme year has ended.

BENEFITS TO THEME YEAR PARTICIPATION

Working on the theme years and One Book program has been a wonderful way to meet and interact with students and faculty all across the curriculum. From the very first year of the program, I've had the opportunity to witness how a book can bring people together in conversation. For the first seven years of the program, we put together "student-created reading guides." Students would read the book and then meet to put together a guide based on the questions they had from the work. These students then worked as "One Book advocates" throughout the year, promoting the book to their fellow students. Working with these student readers has been my all-time greatest experience as a librarian. Taking down their ideas and hearing their enthusiasm and criticisms is inspiring. There were times they thought the authors were full of it, but they were articulate in their praise and their doubts. The best moment was when one of the students said to me after reading Chris Hedges, "I never think to read nonfiction, but now I will." She also spoke of how before reading his book, she took CNN to be gospel. *War Is a Force that Gives Us Meaning* made her rethink and expand her beliefs and develop critical thinking skills—major goals of the One Book program and of Slow Books in general.

I highly recommend working on these programs, as these kind of experiences with students and faculty are rewarding. But know that having clear goals and assessment data is key.

NOTES

1. John Y. Cole, "One Book Projects Grow in Popularity." *Library of Congress Information Bulletin* 65, no. 1 (2006): 30–31.

2. Ibid.

3. "About the Big Read," *The Big Read*, accessed February 26, 2014, http://www.neabigread.org/about.php.

4. For examples, see Mardi Mahaffy, "In Support of Reading: Reading Outreach Programs at Academic Libraries," *Public Services Quarterly* 5, no. 3 (2009): 163–173; Renée Bosman, John Glover, and Monique Prince, "Growing Adult Readers: Promoting Leisure Reading in Academic Libraries," *Urban Library Journal* 15, no. 1 (2008): 46–58; Heidi Gauder, Joan Giglierano, and Christine H. Schramm, "Porch Reads: Encouraging Recreational Reading among College Students," *College & Undergraduate Libraries* 14, no. 2 (2004): 1–24.

5. IUSB Task Force on General Education, *Report and Recommendations* (South Bend: Indiana University South Bend, 2003), accessed February 3, 2013, https://www.iusb.edu/general-educ/GenEd_RepRec.pdf.

6. Ibid., 15.

6

READERS' ADVISORY IN THE COLLEGE CLASSROOM

Barbara Fister

The decline and fall of reading, particularly among the always-on born-digital generation, is a common lament, encouraged by an influential report from the National Endowment for the Humanities in 2004[1] and another in 2007.[2] The second report, in particular, was framed with a "What about the children?" rhetorical move, sounding the alarm about the risks society faces when young people turn away from reading. "There is a general decline in reading among teenage and adult Americans," poet and then NEA chairman Daniel Gioia wrote in the introduction. "Most alarming, both reading ability and the habit of regular reading have greatly declined among college graduates."[3] He concluded by calling current reading practices "a serious national problem" and adding a warning: "If, at the current pace, America continues to lose the habit of regular reading, the nation will suffer substantial economic, social, and civic setbacks."[4]

The methodology and presentation of this study was criticized by Nancy Kaplan, then executive director of the School of Information Arts and Technology at the University of Baltimore, who claimed it relied on insufficient time series data and distorted the data graphically to dramatize its findings.[5] Dan Cohen, then director of the Roy Rosenzweig Center for History and New Media and currently Director of the Digital Public Library of America, contested the report's supposed inclusion of data about reading digital texts while drawing conclusions that appeared to entirely overlook them.[6] Matthew Kirschenbaum, associate professor of English at the University of Maryland and the associate director of the Maryland Institute for Technology in the Humanities, published an essay in the *Chronicle of Higher Education* pointing out that both online reading and writing were thriving, arguing that these activities were no less immersive, involving, and valuable than reading books for pleasure—while also challenging the strict distinction the NEA drew between voluntary and more purposeful, school- or career-related reading.[7]

In an era when more books are being published than ever in history, a wider variety of reading choices is available to readers than ever before, book-centered social media platforms have attracted millions of members, and more people are engaged in creating and sharing texts than in any past generation, it seems curious that people routinely write obituaries for reading (not unlike predictions of the death of books and libraries) in predictable modes: lachrymose, activist, or techno-determinist: It's tragic that reading is dead. We must do something about it before it's too late. There's nothing to be done because the march of technological progress is an inevitable social disruption.

Librarians at Gustavus Adolphus College in St. Peter, Minnesota, were curious about these frequent claims about young people and reading that often feature, at best, cherry-picked evidence and wanted to learn more from college students about their attitudes toward reading for pleasure. We had heard anecdotally from our students that they are fond of books and enjoy reading (though the number and prolixity of assigned readings are not always included in that warm glow). We have a small browsing collection of popular novels and nonfiction that circulates well and had so routinely fielded questions about where the "fiction section" is (or whether we even had any fiction) from students who were in search of pleasure reading material that we put up signs about how to find fiction in the Library of Congress classification system. Since our anecdotal evidence contradicted the dire warnings of the NEA reports, we had to wonder whether the death of reading among young people was greatly exaggerated.

We took two approaches to finding out. In the fall of 2008, we announced a funded opportunity for a student to collaborate on a research project with a librarian to study undergraduates' attitudes toward reading for pleasure.[8] At the same time, I designed a new course, Books and Culture, a 100-level offering that carried the following catalog description:

> To read the news, you'd think books are on the brink of extinction. The National Endowment for the Arts warns that reading books is in precipitous decline, Apple CEO Steve Jobs has announced that nobody reads anymore, and numerous "experts" tell us members of Gen Y aren't interested in anything that isn't high-tech. Yet nearly 300,000 books are published annually and the number of people using public libraries has doubled in the past ten years. This course will explore books in contemporary culture, the book industry from writers to readers, the intellectual history of reading, and the future of the book.

ABOUT "BOOKS AND CULTURE"

This course was designed for our one-month interim session, a time when both students and faculty are encouraged to explore ideas that fall outside the constraints of the regular curriculum. These courses must have an experiential component and necessarily involve an intensive and immersive schedule. Though students take only one course during the interim session, it meets five days a week for several hours each day. Students must take two of these courses as part of their general education requirements, though many students fulfill the requirement off campus, with career explorations or international travel courses. This interim session is both a break from the usual academic pressures and a chance to explore new subjects and unconventional pedagogies.

Unfortunately, the interim session is also a bit of a bore for librarians. The mood during the January term is relatively relaxed and the library, which is bustling during the fall and spring terms, becomes unusually quiet, partly because students are enjoying a departure from their usual study habits and habitats and partly because so many of our students are off campus. It's a particularly opportune time for librarians to contribute to the general education curriculum, and we have offered a number of different courses over the years. I decided to create this course partly to support students who had expressed interest in books and reading (particularly those who were not majoring in the humanities) and partly to explore whether our anecdotal reports about enthusiasm for reading were widely shared or anomalies. Early indications were positive. This was the first of our interim courses, with an enrollment cap of 25, to completely fill during the first day of registration—and once it was full, emails poured in requesting permission to join the course, some from students who had already fulfilled the two-course requirement but wanted to take the course regardless. Ultimately, 29 students completed the course. As of this writing, the course has been offered two more times, enrolling 32 and 36 students.[9]

The unanticipated enthusiasm with which this course was met spurred our interest in studying student attitudes toward reading for pleasure. In the spring of 2009, Amara Berthelsen, the student researcher selected to work with librarian Julie Gilbert, conducted a campus-wide study asking about student attitudes toward reading, reading practices, and perceived barriers to reading for pleasure. The survey population was recruited by targeting courses at all levels across the curriculum and securing the collaboration of a number of faculty who were willing to surrender class time for administration of the survey. This in-class distribution of the survey instrument ensured that results were representative of the student body, regardless of their reading attitudes and experiences, and captured a representative cross-section of majors and genders, with nearly a third of our students participating. (It should be noted that, though Gustavus is a liberal arts college, data obtained from first-year students who participated in the Wabash National Study of Liberal Arts Education suggested that they are not more likely than students at other kinds of institutions to read for pleasure, at least at the time they enter college. The study included students enrolled in a variety of institutions, including community colleges and research universities.[10] This is consistent with other studies that found reading for pleasure more popular with students than is generally surmised.[11]) Simultaneously, we conducted a survey of academic librarians and a very limited survey of faculty in other disciplines to gauge their impressions of undergraduates' reading habits and preferences.[12]

One surprising finding of the surveys was that our students expressed a much greater interest in reading for pleasure than the librarians or faculty we surveyed had predicted. A vast majority of students—93 percent—reported that they enjoy leisure reading, with general fiction the most popular reading choice. (This, of course, is the kind of reading the NEA claimed was particularly endangered.) A smaller majority of students also reported enjoying reading newspapers and magazines. The Internet was the least likely source for leisure reading material, though we suspect respondents may have failed to include use of social media in their interpretation of this option. There were intriguing gender differences in expressed reading preferences, with women more likely than men to express interest in general fiction, classics, mysteries, and romance; men expressed more interest than women in science fiction and Internet-based sources.

The academic librarians and faculty surveyed as part of the study were not as sanguine about students' interest in reading. Around 40 percent of librarians and faculty reported that they felt students simply weren't very interested in reading for pleasure. This belief may have been influenced by the despairing reports in the popular press about the decline of reading among youth, or it may have been based on accurate observation. Another finding of our student survey is that, though nearly all students said they enjoy reading for pleasure, nearly all also report they do very little of it during the school year, explaining in their comments, "After homework, it's hard to read for fun," "NO TIME!" and "Not enough physical hours in the day to do much else but go to class, do homework and occasionally sleep." Paradoxically, though reading assigned in class may provide excellent training in critical reading strategies, it might also (because it is so relentless and voluminous) interfere with students' ability to develop a sense of what they personally enjoy reading and to acquire routine strategies for discovering reading material on their own. When they graduate, they may be skilled at reading but underprepared for making the individual choices that sustain a lifelong reading habit. They may also identify libraries as primarily a place to study and librarians as advisors for academic tasks rather than as allies in making choices that satisfy and develop their lifelong personal reading tastes.

This seems at the very least to be a lost opportunity. Institutions of higher education routinely make claims about preparing students for lifelong learning, and libraries frequently frame information literacy as essential preparation for lifetime engagement with ideas and self-directed learning, yet we do little to encourage our students to include public library membership in their postgraduation plans, nor do we do much to prepare students to make use of information that isn't sought in response to a clearly articulated academic need. Indeed, the *Information Literacy Competency Standards for Higher Education* (which was adopted in 2000 and is under revision as of this writing), seem based on the assumption that patterns of information use mimic the process of writing papers for college, assuming, for example, that the information-literate individual begins the process of using information by first defining a need for it. Catherine Sheldrick Ross pointed out in the same year that the standards were adopted that much of the information people use in their daily lives, information that informs their view of the world and their sense of identity, is not sought but rather is encountered, often through pleasure reading.[13] Most information literacy instruction is (understandably) geared to the immediate and practical need that students have to complete tasks that they did not initiate themselves. Though this approach does much to integrate learning into course goals and taps into student motivation, it does little to help students develop an instinct for encountering information through self-directed curiosity and enjoyment. The Books and Culture course uniquely addresses this problem. In giving students the time, freedom, and skills to explore their own reading tastes, this course enables them to pursue their own curiosity and thus to be lifelong learners—the ultimate goal of both information literacy and higher education.

There is compelling evidence that reading for pleasure has benefits that align well with information literacy goals. Research on readers (particularly of fiction) has found that reading enhances empathy[14] and creativity,[15] provides more insight into social issues than scholarly research does,[16] is a vehicle for the acquisition of general knowledge,[17] and affirms identity while also providing readers with a greater appreciation of life experiences different from their own.[18] Surely, these benefits should be nurtured as part of a college education.

READING IN THE CLASSROOM, PART 2: INTRODUCING THE "READING WORKSHOP"

To help students who profess a love of reading while claiming they have little time for it, we proposed a second book-focused credit-bearing course, one that would fit into the regular semester (and our workload) and would be attractive to busy students. It offers a small amount of credit and little risk as an incentive to students who want to read but who feel it competes with academic demands that have a higher priority. Basing our concept on partial-credit courses that promote lifelong fitness, we proposed a single-credit pass/fail course to make it an attractive, yet low-stakes, addition to busy schedules. Yet, to avoid it seeming too elementary, we gave it a 200-level designation, explaining in our course proposal, "We want it to be open to all students through the senior year; the 200 level is intended to suggest it won't be too elementary for seniors or too hard for motivated first year students." We also made sure that both the timing of the course (late afternoon in the first half of the spring semester) and the amount of credit offered would attract students without overloading their schedules during crunch time and without increasing their tuition bill, as most students would be able to add it to a full load without incurring additional fees.

The course proposal form requires a rationale for each new course, including how it fits into the long-range instructional goals of the department and the institution. This is how we made a case for the course, which we titled Reading Workshop:

> Our Lindell Scholarship research project in Spring 2009 included a survey on students' attitudes toward reading. We learned that the majority of students (> 90%) say they enjoy reading and they would read more if they had the time. We see this course as a kind of intellectual fitness course, offering students a scheduled time and a small amount of academic credit to read and discuss books and other texts (newspapers, magazines such as The New Yorker); we also see it as a way to encourage lifelong reading by giving students an opportunity to think about their own reading and about literacy practices beyond required reading in college. This issue of how what we in the library contribute to student learning after college is one that we find particularly pressing, and we hope this course will help students build a bridge from pre-college reading to post-college literacy habits, including developing personal strategies for discovering books of interest (a skill that several studies indicate has a strong influence on whether or not people choose to read voluntarily). Our plan is to eventually offer two or more of these short courses each year with the books that each section will read publicized in advance so that students can choose a discussion they want to join. We will select books for spring 2011 in early fall and publicize choices before the registration period. Though we haven't selected books yet, we would consider books such as *The Omnivore's Dilemma* by Michael Pollan, *Zeitoun* by Dave Eggers, or *The Immortal Life of Henrietta Lacks* by Rebecca Skloot.

The proposal form also asks whether the course might duplicate offerings of another department. We responded:

> We don't see this as competing in any way with literature courses offered by the English or MLLC [Modern Languages, Literatures, and Cultures] departments because we are not focusing as much on learning how to read or about a particular body of literature so much as helping students be reflective about their own reading practices and about the role of books and reading in society.

The course was approved by the Curriculum Committee in the fall of 2010 and was first offered in the spring semester of 2011. It has been offered every spring since then.

As every academic librarian who has offered a credit-bearing elective course knows, offering a course is one thing; getting students to enroll in it is another. Though Reading Workshop is listed in the course catalog, there is little reason a student planning his or her registration would discover it. It lives with a motley handful of courses in a nondepartmental no-man's land. Though we market the course during spring registration through our website and with posters, we've found the best word of mouth comes from faculty advisors who encourage students to enroll either because they think it's a worthwhile experience or because some of their advisees need a small amount of additional credit to meet requirements for graduation—or both. We reach out to departments and to individual faculty who we think may recommend the course, particularly if the book chosen for discussion is relevant to their subject area. Faculty, once contacted, often continue to promote the course year after year.

The outcomes for students as stated in the syllabus are to learn:

- The value of reading and discussing books, even when they are not required
- How to analyze your own reading preferences
- Some practical means of discovering books you are likely to enjoy
- A little bit about the role that books and reading play in society

These outcomes are encouraged by involving students in informal discussion of a common book (including asking them to take turns leading discussion), engaging them in free writing exercises that analyze their reading history and preferences, having them select a book to read and review, contributing their reviews to a "students recommend" catalog maintained on LibraryThing, and exploring various freely available readers advisory tools[19] (and practicing readers advisory amongst ourselves). At the end of the course, students use the readers' advisory tools we have introduced and suggestions from fellow students to compile a list of 10 books they might want to read in the future. Students also experience reading as a social activity by contributing to discussion guides for the books we read together and by sharing their book reviews both in class and publicly.

Although these course outcomes are not aligned in an obvious way with the current *Information Literacy Standards* (and, in fact, were designed in part to thwart students' usual approaches to the library as a place to find useful information for their assignments, instead encouraging personal exploration and pleasure), one could say learning how to discover reading material that one enjoys is a means of understanding and articulating an "information need," broadening what we mean when we talk about "information." Students encounter and use tools that will help them explore their options and make personally satisfying choices, which is a nonacademic way of designing a search strategy and evaluating sources. They practice, through discussion, interpreting information through analysis and discourse with others. They create a "product" (though it's unlikely they would use that term to describe the book reviews they write and share), they query how their reading fits into their personal knowledge base, and they consider ethical uses of information, including providing a citation that will help others locate the reviewed work and honoring a tenant of popular book reviewing: no spoilers! Though our learning outcomes were not drawn up with the *Standards* in mind, the kind of learning that is being promoted enacts them—and, perhaps, shows how they can be applied to day-to-day information use after college.

The first time the Reading Workshop was offered, we wanted to choose a book that would appeal to science majors, who constitute a large portion of the student population and seemed least likely to have opportunities for pleasurable reading in their courses. We chose Rebecca Skloot's *The Immortal Life of Henrietta Lacks,* which offered great potential for discussion and had appeal for students in all majors. In addition to discussing the book, we watched Adam Curtis's 1997 documentary, *The Way of All Flesh*, which is mentioned in the book. We also invited faculty to join us for refreshments and conversation on the last day of discussion. Since then, we have discussed *Zeitoun* by Dave Eggers and *Reservation Blues* by Sherman Alexie. In the spring of 2014, the discussion book was Amy Chua's *Battle Hymn of the Tiger Mother,* which offers opportunities to discuss parenting, childhood, and contested cultural values that inform family dynamics.

Even though we have taken care to make the course accessible, it has not attracted the same level of interest as our interim term course. Enrollment is capped at 15 to promote discussion but, even so, it doesn't always fill. We originally planned to offer two sections annually but found that there wasn't enough enrollment to justify librarians' time. It's not entirely clear why it isn't more popular, given that student feedback has been consistently positive. We can only speculate that even though we were careful to make it possible to fit our reading assignments into busy schedules, it still is seen as time and effort that competes with the demands of courses in the major. Unlike the interim term course, it doesn't fulfill any general education requirement other than the need to accumulate a certain number of credits to graduate. It's somewhat hidden in the course catalog, whereas all of the interim experience courses are described in a single menu-style document. It may also be the case that students associate pleasure reading with a part of the annual academic calendar that they associate with fun and freedom, whereas the spring term is a time to be serious and focus on academics. There is also more competition in terms of social options. Student organizations and campus activities are livelier in the spring semester than in January.

Though enrollments have not been particularly strong, suggesting that even offering credit isn't sufficient incentive for students to make time to read for pleasure during the semester, the students who take the course have received it warmly. It has attracted a diverse group of students, some of whom are avid readers who have no trouble developing a "to be read" list and others who are just beginning to explore their taste in books. Course evaluations indicate that they appreciate the opportunity to discuss books in a relaxed and informal setting. They report that this experience is quite different than other course discussions, which emphasize close reading of challenging literature or critical analysis of scholarly research. Some of the students find the open-endedness of discussion a little too unstructured for their tastes, which is an issue that bears further scrutiny. Though many courses at Gustavus emphasize discussion, it is often heavily guided, framed with preclass writing assignments or preset discussion prompts. We feel the informality and relatively unstructured nature of our discussions is good practice for self-directed reading and discussion after college, but we may need to find ways to ensure students have opportunities to develop a sense of ownership of the discussions.

Though the kind of learning that pleasure reading promotes doesn't fit neatly into the *Information Literacy Competency Standards* developed in 2000,[20] which tend to emphasize information seeking performed in connection with producing scholarship, we feel that the self-directed exploration readers experience is a valuable kind of learning and that it should also be practiced and rewarded. Courses like Books and Culture and the Reading Workshop do just that. Although literally rewarding students with academic credit, these courses also reward students by giving them both the time and freedom to develop their personal taste in reading as well as the information literacy skills needed to pursue it. Helping students develop their personal taste in reading—and a taste *for* reading—is critical preparation for lifelong learning.

NOTES

1. National Endowment for the Arts, *Reading at Risk: A Survey of Literary Reading in America* (Washington, D.C.: National Endowment for the Arts, 2004), http://www.nea.gov/pub/ReadingAtRisk.pdf.

2. National Endowment for the Arts, *To Read or Not to Read: A Question of National Consequence* (Washington, D.C.: National Endowment for the Arts, 2007), http://arts.endow.gov/research/ToRead.pdf.

3. National Endowment for the Arts, *To Read or Not to Read,* pp. 5–6.

4. Ibid.

5. Nancy Kaplan, "Reading Responsibly: Nancy Kaplan on the NEA's Data Distortion," *If:book* (blog), November 30, 2007 (11:05 p.m.), http://futureofthebook.org/blog/2007/11/30/reading_responsibly_nancy_kaplan/.

6. Dan Cohen, "The Digital Critique of 'To Read or Not to Read,'" *Dan Cohen* (blog) January 10, 2008, http://www.dancohen.org/2008/01/10/the-digital-critique-of-to-read-or-not-to-read/.

7. Matthew Kirschenbaum, "How Reading Is Being Reimagined," *Chronicle of Higher Education*, December 7, 2007, https://chronicle.com/article/How-Reading-Is-Being/17111.

8. The survey research was funded by an endowment provided by Gustavus Library Associates, a friend-of-the-library group. Every other year, they fund a generous stipend for a student to conduct research with a librarian. This program is called the Lindell Scholarship after Patricia Lindell, the founder of the fundraising group.

9. The most recent course syllabus, class notes, slide deck, and assignment prompts, all available for reuse and remixing under a Creative Commons NC-BY license, may be found at http://booksandculture13.wordpress.com.

10. Though data specific to Gustavus students are not publicly available, information about the study and participating institutions can be found in the "Wabash National Study at a Glance," Center of Inquiry in the Liberal Arts, accessed January 24, 2014, http://www.liberalarts.wabash.edu/storage/WNS_description.pdf.

11. See, for example, Charlene Blackwood et al., "Pleasure Reading by College Students: Fact or Fiction?" (paper presented at the Annual Meeting of the Mid-South Educational Research Association, Lexington,KY, November 13–15, 1991, ERIC ED344191); Kouider Mokhtari, Carla A. Reichard, and Anne Gardner, "The Impact of Internet and Television Use on the Reading Habits and Practices of College Students," *Journal of Adolescent & Adult Literacy* 52, no. 7 (April 2009): 609–619; Allison Hari and David A. Joliffe, "Texts of Our Institutional Lives: Studying the 'Reading Transition' from High School to College: What Are Our Students Reading and Why?" *College English* 70, no. 6 (July 2008): 600

12. The survey instruments and results can be found in Julie Gilbert and Barbara Fister, "Reading Risk and Reality: College Students and Reading for Pleasure," *College & Research Libraries* 72, no. 5 (2011): 490, http://crl.acrl.org/content/72/5/474.full.pdf+html.

13. Catherine Sheldrick Ross, "Finding without Seeking: What Readers Say about the Role of Pleasure Reading as a Source of Information," *Australasian Public Libraries and Information Services* 13, no. 2 (June 2000): 72–80.

14. Raymond A. Mar and Keith Oatley, "The Function of Fiction Is the Abstraction and Simulation of Social Experience," *Perspectives on Psychological Science* 3, no. 3 (2008): 173–192.

15. Kathryn E. Kelly and Lee B. Kneipp, "Reading for Pleasure and Creativity among College Students," *College Student Journal* 43, no. 4 (December 2009): 1137–1144; Jessica Moyer, "Learning from Leisure Reading: A Study of Public Library Patrons," *Reference and Users Services Quarterly* 46, no. 4 (2007): 66–79.

16. David Lewis, Dennis Rodgers, and Michael Woolcock, "The Fiction of Development: Literary Representation as a Source of Authoritative Knowledge," *Journal of Development Studies* 44, no. 2 (2008): 198–216.

17. Richard Gerrig, *Experiencing Narrative Worlds: On the Psychology of Reading for Pleasure* (Boulder, CO: Westview, 1998).

18. Research on the role of reading in identity formation is amply explored in Catherine Sheldrick Ross, Lynne (E. F.) McKechnie, and Paulette M Rothbauer, eds., *Reading Matters: What the Research Reveals about Reading, Libraries, and Community* (Westport, CT: Libraries Unlimited, 2006).

19. For example, "Literature-Map," Gnod, accessed April 9, 2014, http://www.literature-map.com/; "Whichbook," Opening the Book, accessed April 9, 2014, http://www.openingthebook.com/whichbook/; "Stop, You're Killing Me!" accessed April 9, 2014, http://www.stopyourekillingme.com/; "What's Next," Kent District Library, accessed April 9, 2014, http://ww2.kdl.org/libcat/whatsnext.asp; "Fiction_L Booklists,"

Morton Grove Public Library, accessed April 9, 2014, http://www.mgpl.org/read-listen-view/fl/flbooklists/.

20. Association of College and Research Libraries, *Information Literacy Competency Standards*, last modified January, 18, 2000, accessed December 13, 2013, http://www.ala.org/acrl/standards/informationliteracycompetency. As of this writing, the *Standards* are being thoroughly revised.

7

REVISITING THE DORMITORY: THE RPS LIBRARIES OF INDIANA UNIVERSITY

Willie Miller

From the perspective of a typical undergraduate college student, life does not open itself to many extracurricular reading opportunities. When I was an undergraduate, juggling classwork, membership in campus organizations, friends, family, and a part-time job meant I did not always complete assigned readings, never mind enjoyable reading. In graduate school at Indiana University, I was exposed to what seemed like a fantastical idea—residence hall libraries to support leisure reading. Now, I am convinced that having a library full of classic and contemporary literature, films, music, and more in the dormitory, so close students do not have to change out of pajama pants and slippers to go, is an excellent way to associate reading with pleasure for undergraduate students and to create a campus culture of reading.

HISTORY OF DORMITORY LIBRARIES

Little has been written on the topic; yet, it is known that history owes the concept and subsequent popularization of the residence hall library to the House Library Plan at Harvard University. Opening with seven residential libraries in 1928, the houses of Harvard created picturesque study spaces and academic collections under the supervision of a resident "master."[1] The objective behind the house libraries was to integrate living and learning and "to restore to undergraduate life some of the social values it had [once] offered . . ."[2] The house masters curated a collection of books to directly support academic coursework, which were checked in and out on the honor system.[3] The overall goal can be seen in the description of the Lowell House Library, "a scholarly gentleman's library to appeal to literary tastes and to encourage potential bibliophiles."[4] Gradually, individual house libraries developed subject specialties. For example, some would cater more to students of the humanities, while others focused in the sciences.[5]

Following the Harvard House Plan, many institutions experimented with the model of residence hall libraries. At the peak of the trend (roughly 1940–1960), there were more than 20 residence hall library systems across North America. Among them were operations at Harvard University, Stephens College, Yale University, Dartmouth University, Iowa State University, Michigan State University, Pennsylvania State University, Stanford University, Syracuse University, Princeton University, University of Alberta, University of California at Los Angeles, University of Kansas, University of Michigan, University of Illinois at Urbana-Champaign, and Indiana University.[6]

Residence hall libraries were difficult for institutions to operate for various reasons, including management, funding, and security.[7, 8, 9] Edward Stanford found that oversight by the university library system was essential to the success of a residence hall library; however, many systems still struggled with the question of which unit should manage the residence libraries.[10] Along with the problem of management was the problem of sustainable funding. The creation of a new library system required institutions to invest a considerable amount of money without a clear indication of the outcome.[11] Finally, with Harvard's model for circulation control operating on the honor system amid limited staffing, many subsequent residence hall libraries failed because of theft. One librarian decried, "Without regular staffing these [collections] were all looted and scattered indiscriminately. . . . unless these [residence hall libraries] are set up as staffed and controlled collections. . . . it is not worth investing money in them . . ."[12]

By 1978, the number of active residence hall libraries funded and serving students had shrunk to 12.[13] In 2014, that number has further shriveled to two: University of Illinois at Urbana-Champaign and Indiana University. While residence halls at Stanford and Yale still offer libraries in their lists of amenities, these facilities are not staffed, nor are their collections listed in the university catalog. Additionally, the University of Michigan maintained residence hall libraries until the 2003–2004 academic year, at which time they started converting some libraries into community learning centers and deaccessioned or sold the contents of the others.[14]

Opening in 1969, the residence hall libraries at the University of Illinois at Urbana-Champaign have had a successful history due to a full-time staff and institutional support. This program moved beyond the limits of the initial Harvard model and adapted to serve users with the best methods possible. Nevertheless, this chapter will focus on the older and larger residence hall library system at Indiana University in Bloomington. As a graduate student in the IU School of Library and Information Science, I worked in this system of residence hall libraries. During my tenure, I worked at each location, starting as a student assistant, then a center supervisor, and eventually the assistant manager of libraries.

HALLS OF RESIDENCE LIBRARIES AT INDIANA UNIVERSITY

The Indiana University residence hall libraries have a long and complicated history, which is best chronicled by Barbara Brand Fischler[15] and David A. Flynn.[16] Susan Andriette Ariew[17] and Gail Oltmanns and John H. Schuh[18] also track the system's journey and impact. When the first residence hall library opened what was then Men's Residence Living Center (now the Collins Living-Learning Center) in February 1941, the residence hall libraries were a kind of souvenir brought back by the eleventh president of Indiana University, Herman B Wells, and the director of the halls of residence, Alice Nelson, from individual trips to the dormitory libraries at Harvard and Yale.[19] Wells is noted as saying, "... if something was good enough for Yale or Harvard or Princeton, it might be good enough for us."[20] The impetus of the Halls of Residence Libraries, as it would soon be called, was the thought that there is a positive educational advantage to leisure-time reading in student housing, and this would be beneficial to student learning and success.[21] More than 70 years later, this foundational idea still supports the IU system of residence hall libraries.

Funding the Halls of Residence Libraries initiated substantial cultural change at the university. On October 1, 1940, the Halls of Residence Committee voted to allow vending machines in the dormitories for the first time and to use a portion of the revenue to purchase books for the new libraries.[22] By January 1, 1941, purchases from the new candy, peanut, cigarette, and Coca-Cola machines reached $505.05, enabling the new libraries to get off of the ground.[23] Collection development for the libraries was led by two committees of faculty members and students who represented the residence hall population. Each residence hall created a list of suggested items, and the student representatives presented the lists to the committees for approval.[24] The first list of titles included *Birds of America, Encyclopedia of Art, Physics Made Easy, Book of Oriental Literature, Nine Plays, Origin of Species*, and *War and Peace*.[25] Though the consensus was that the Halls of Residence Libraries should not be reference rooms for university courses, the committees were concerned with stocking shelves with "good" leisure-time reading "... to develop the student's desire to know good books."[26]

As the Halls of Residence Libraries expanded both in number and collections, the concept of "good" materials would clash with students' desires for recreational reading. When in 1945 IU band director Gerald H. Doty was chosen to lead a committee to develop a music collection that would provide "permanent value" to the residence hall libraries, he concluded "this would eliminate all popular purchases from [the] fund."[27] This struggle between "good" or high-caliber items and popular items continued as the collection expanded into film. The Halls of Residence Committee chose only films "of an educational nature and not for recreational type of entertainment."[28]

The management of the Halls of Residence Libraries has been the responsibility of many units over the years. Starting with the Residence Halls Committee with a brief period of collaboration with the University Libraries, the system was also managed by the Graduate School and the dean of students. Mismanagement seriously bungled the system's collection development and infrastructure. Similar to other dormitory library systems, many items were lost and stolen from the libraries at IU.

In 1959, the dean of undergraduate development, Samuel Braden, hired the first full-time HRL librarian, Barbara Pratt.[29] During her tenure, the legendary Pratt whipped the system into shape. She started a tradition of hiring graduate Library and Information Science (LIS) students to manage each individual library. In addition, she opened new libraries and instituted a new collection development plan—one that valued student interest a bit more than prestige. Doris Koch, Pratt's long-time assistant, recalls, "[We] saw a basic Rock 'n Roll collection listed in one of the library journals and we bought the whole thing for each library. . . . We sort of agonized over whether to buy eight-tracks or cassettes. . . . we chose the cassettes."[30] This is a far cry from the planned music collection of 1945.

Decreasing vending machine revenue accompanied by the allowance of low-watt mini-fridges in dorm rooms signaled a necessary change to the Halls of Residence Libraries. Following much discussion, the system's management moved into the control of the University Libraries in 1974, and funding was provided from a three-dollar activity fee added to tuition costs.[31] In the hands of the University Libraries and under the direction of Carolyn Tynan Walters, the system opened a family housing library and added the collection of 30,000 materials to the online university catalog.[32]

MOVE FROM IU LIBRARIES TO RPS AND CURRENT STRUCTURE

In 2001, Halls of Residence Libraries was moved under the control of IU Residential Programs and Services (RPS).[33] However, the new RPS Libraries maintained collaboration with the University Libraries through sustained connection of the latter's circulation and cataloging infrastructure. At this time, six previous library spaces were converted into Music, Movies, and More (3M) centers to complement the other six, more successful, residential libraries. When former libraries were renovated into 3M centers, their monograph collections were added to the remaining libraries' collections, and RPS leaders made sure that a full library was located in every residence neighborhood on campus; therefore, residential students would always be within walking distance of an RPS library. Administratively, the system sits under the control of the director of residential life, and Manager of Academic Services Shawn Wilson, who holds a master of library science degree, is the manager of libraries.

In addition to Wilson, the RPS Libraries central office employs Library Services Coordinator Tina Walsh, an assistant manager of libraries, a part-time cataloger, and two student technical assistants. Each of the 12 libraries and 3M centers has a center supervisor, usually a graduate student in library science, and a staff of five to seven student assistants. Locations are open 5:00 p.m. until midnight, seven nights a week during the regular academic year. The system is closed during school breaks, and only the Campus View (Family Housing) Library operates during the summer.

In the 2012–2013 academic year, 111,450 users visited the libraries. This number is usually higher; however, one 3M was closed during the year for renovations. As of February 2014, the Indiana University online catalog, IUCAT, showed RPS Libraries holdings of 49,700 items. The system circulates books (reference, fiction, and nonfiction), music (CDs), films (DVDs & Blu-ray), and various video games, and all libraries offer a noncirculating collection of popular newspapers and magazines. Student identification cards serve as library cards, and fines are connected to a student's bursar account balance. With a staff of about 90 and 49 weekly open hours, the RPS Libraries system is similar to a small public library system.

POPULAR COLLECTIONS

Beginning in 1949 with the construction of the Joseph A. Wright Quadrangle, every new residence hall on the IU Bloomington campus had space for a library.[34] In many dorms, Willkie Residence Center, for example, the library space is a beautiful and prominent feature of the architecture. Currently, every library has shelving adequate to hold roughly 6,000 materials (books, DVDs, CDs, newspapers, and magazines), study tables and chairs, soft seating, and a circulation desk. The 3M centers are smaller spaces that are not designed for study. The libraries and 3M centers are near enough to residence hall computer labs that most do not have computers available for users.

The residence hall libraries of Indiana University, Bloomington were established as a source of "good leisure reading and reference materials."[35] During its history, "good leisure reading" has had many meanings. In 1941, it seemed to mean "of lasting educational value." Seventy-three years later, more worth is placed on the value of pleasurable, popular, and/or culturally significant materials. Indeed, the times have changed, and films need not be purely educational—both entertainment and cultural impact are considered important.

After a study of students' use and perceptions of the residence hall libraries, IU librarian Gail Oltmanns and Associate Dean of Students John H. Schuh found data to suggest collections of this type should be developed more to meet the recreational reading needs of students.[36] Oltmanns and Schuh conclude successful residence hall libraries "should meet the general public library needs of students who live in residence, and that academic needs can be met by. . . . the campus library system."[37] The current mission of RPS Libraries is to provide "residents with library collections, programs, and services that support their academic, cultural, and recreational needs."[38] It is perhaps the support of recreational needs that is most responsible for the continued success of the system.

The direction of the collection development in the RPS Libraries has tilted into the direction of popular materials since at least the Pratt era. This is reasonable since the system is motivated by use: from 1974 to present, residential student activity fees have funded the system, and low door counts would signal its obsolescence. By filling a gap in the collections of the main university library system and being more convenient than the local public library to residential students, the RPS Libraries niche of popular items ensures its success. Many a graduate student and faculty member has been saddened to learn that all of the university's copies of, say, *Mean Girls* are owned by RPS Libraries and are available only to residents of the residence halls, though the system will allow a professor to check out materials for class under special permission. Even at a time when Redbox, Netflix, iTunes, Kindles, and illegal downloading are ubiquitous, the RPS libraries are as busy as ever.

This is not to say the collections of the RPS Libraries are trivial in nature. The holdings of the system include reference books, classic literature, award-winning films, and music. In the very early years, it would have been unlikely for contemporary literature to be purchased; however, current collection development relies on sources like the *New York Times*, Amazon, and iTunes for their bestseller's lists. Residence hall libraries previously contained reserves for courses, but this service is no longer provided. It likely ended after Oltmanns and Schuh's study on the use of the libraries. The system relieved itself of most services that competed against the university libraries' expertise, though it should not be said that the RPS Libraries directly competes with the local public library, and the Monroe County Public Library remains a very successful library system. Further, staff encourage users to patronize the public library if they cannot find desired items within the RPS Libraries holdings. In this way, the system helps inspire students to use the public library and to build a habit of library use for life.

As previously mentioned, monographic purchase decisions take into account resources such as the *New York Times* and Amazon's bestseller lists. The libraries aim to offer books that are popular in contemporary culture, in addition to literary classics and genre fiction. In this way, the collections are similar to "browsing collections," which are becoming a trend in traditional academic libraries.[39] Broadening into public library territory, staff members of the RPS Libraries provide readers' and/or viewers' advisory services. Moreover, locations most often feature a "staff picks" display with book, movie, or album reviews written by student assistants and center supervisors.

EMBEDDED LIBRARIANSHIP

Though there is a considerable amount of overlap, each library's collection maintains a personality of its own, largely based on each dormitory's student population. For example, the Campus View (Family Housing) Library serves more international students than average and as a result, its collection has a significant number of international and foreign language items. Additionally, as it serves families, the Campus View Library is the only RPS library with children's books. The Collins Library is known for its collection of graphic novels and zines, as the students of the Collins Living-Learning Center are known for their creative and artistic talents.

Moreover, in most cases, a residence hall's student government makes special donations to the library or 3M to expand its collection to include materials of educational or cultural significance to students in residence. In 2009, the students of Eigenmann Residence Center gave such a donation to start a collection of books on the topic of sustainability. The center supervisor not only purchased materials in the area but also collaborated with student organizations to develop programs on the topic of environmental sustainability in the library.

Collaboration with the residence hall is important to the staff of the RPS Libraries. The move in management from the University Libraries to Residential Programs and Services seems to have added powerful motivation to work with residence hall staff and student organizations. Center supervisors sit on the community boards of the residence centers and often collaborate with center constituents to provide relevant, cohesive programming. The library system is completely embedded in the residence hall, and it is successful as a result of the full support of the residential life unit.

In addition, each month, center supervisors are required to develop an outreach program. RPS Libraries management encourages partnerships with campus or residence hall organizations. Monthly programs usually highlight a part of the location's collection, and they have educational, cultural, and/or recreational learning outcomes. Some past programs include Banned Books, Hispanic History, and Love & Murder (Valentine's Day). A successful program RPS libraries have offered is one in which a user reads a certain number of books from the collection or possibly even from a specific genre. After completing the readings, the user receives a candy bar. This kind of programming helps build a more robust culture of reading on campus and creates a community of readers within the residence hall. Further, possibly nostalgic of primary school, users of the RPS Libraries respond well to programs with a crafting component, and accordingly, many programs feature craft projects like creating hand turkeys, coloring, and origami. Most RPS Libraries staff believe the crafting programs are playful pastimes to help students relax from coursework.

THE POTENTIAL OF RESIDENCE HALL LIBRARIES

Recent literature on libraries and residence halls highlights successful instances of academic library outreach in residence centers, with notable programs at Purdue University and the University of Oklahoma.[40, 41, 42] Moreover, some chapters of this book detail the development and triumph of small community lending libraries in residence halls. These initiatives are significant and should be esteemed; however, it is my belief that these are only small steps toward a far away goal. If the literature is true, and academic librarians want students, particularly undergraduate students, to engage in more pleasure reading, then academic libraries need to reconsider the residence hall library in the model of Indiana University or the University of Illinois at Urbana-Champaign.

The trend of popular browsing collections at academic libraries is surging. Academic librarians are asserting the importance of leisure reading collections, which include popular titles students would want to read for pleasure.[43] This trend is partially steeped in the belief that students will be attracted to the popular items and will perhaps also peruse more of the library's collection.[44] However, a major obstacle to this movement is the cadre of academic librarians who fear popular browsing areas will somehow make academic libraries appear less academic and more like a public library.[45] Creating a residence hall branch library and relocating a potential popular browsing collection to that space could be a solution to assuage concerns and increase student engagement with the main campus library.

Students are more likely to engage in pleasure reading when engaged in an academic setting.[46] For recreation, they are more likely to use visual media than books.[47] The RPS library model for collections, which feature books, movies, music, and more, capitalizes not only on the media preferences of undergraduate students it also creates an environment conducive to pleasure reading. A common display at an RPS library will center on a popular movie or television series. The message will advertise, "Do you like the *Twilight* films? You might also enjoy the *Twilight* series of books. Or *Buffy the Vampire Slayer*. Or Bram Stoker's *Dracula*. Or books by Anne Rice. Or the latest album by Vampire Weekend." All of the suggested items would be on display and available, and based on my experience, most of the items would be circulated. This kind of readers' and viewers' advisory is uncomfortable for many academic librarians,[48] but it does feel natural in a residence hall library.

If an institution were to create a new residence hall library, it would be important to collaborate with the director of residence life. The university library and the office of student affairs could negotiate a funding structure. The idea could be proposed as a joint initiative to increase retention and academic success. The expertise in the academic library's circulation and security infrastructure would be essential to protect the investment in the collection. As a potential branch of the main library system, such a library could feature some small reference services and guides. In addition to print books, a residence hall library would do well to include popular eBooks.

Furthermore, it seems imperative for residence hall libraries to be open late night and weekend hours. The most active time for an RPS library is Friday night, when more than 100 students enter the doors in search of a productive way to relax. Both IU and UIUC have success employing trained student workers to staff the libraries during open hours.

Though a residence hall library is not the answer for every institution, it would likely work on many campuses. The 86–year-old idea "to encourage potential bibliophiles"[49] is still a good one, though its initial conception was flawed. The flaws included poor security, mismanagement, and spotty, uninteresting collections. The final flaw was a tragic result of the residence hall library attempting to compete with the main academic library. Competition for dominance in academic collections, course reserves, and reference will never and has never been the appropriate fight for the residence hall library. On the other hand, the residence hall library can extraordinarily provide a niche collection in popular titles to support or augment a student's academic, cultural, and recreational needs. Instead of competing with the public library, it brings the public library to a demographic that traditionally does not use it or read for pleasure.

NOTES

1. Kenneth Morgan, "The Harvard House Libraries." *Library Journal* 56, no. 6 (June 15 1931): 536–539.
2. Frank N. Jones, "The Libraries of the Harvard Houses." *Harvard Library Bulletin* 2 (Autumn 1948), 362.
3. Susan Andriette Ariew, "The Failure of the Open Access Residence Hall Library," *College and Research Libraries* 39, no. 5 (1978): 372–380, http://crl.acrl.org/content/39/5/372.full.pdf+html.
4. Frank N. Jones, "The Libraries of the Harvard Houses," *Harvard Library Bulletin* 2 (Autumn 1948), 363.
5. Edward B. Stanford, "Residence Hall Libraries and Their Educational Potential," *College and Research Libraries* 30, no. 3 (1969), 198, http://crl.acrl.org/content/30/3/197.full.pdf+html.
6. Ariew, "The Failure of the Open Access Residence Hall Library," 373–374.
7. Stanford, "Residence Hall Libraries and Their Educational Potential," 197–203.
8. Ariew, "The Failure of the Open Access Residence Hall Library," 372–380.
9. Gail V. Oltmanns and John H Schuh, "Purposes and Uses of Residence Hall Libraries," *College & Research Libraries* 46, no. 2 (1985): 172–177, http://crl.acrl.org/content/46/2/172.full.pdf+html.
10. Stanford, "Residence Hall Libraries and Their Educational Potential," 197–203.
11. Ibid., 201.
12. Ibid., 202.
13. Andriette Ariew, "The Failure of the Open Access Residence Hall Library," 374.
14. Eleanor Fye, Ke Lu, and Jennifer Sharp. "Finding Aid for Residence Hall Libraries (University of Michigan) Records, 1954–2005." *University of Michigan Archives*, last modified November 2013, accessed February 24, 2014, http://quod.lib.umich.edu/b/bhlead/umich-bhl-90170?rgn=main;view=text.

15. Barbara Brand Fischler, "An Analysis of the Use of the Undergraduate Halls of Residence Libraries at Indiana University" (master's thesis, Indiana University, 1964), 1–34.

16. David A. Flynn, "There's No Place Like Home: A History of the Halls of Residence Libraries at Indiana University, Bloomington." *Indiana Libraries* 12, no. 1 (1993): 2–10.

17. Ariew, "The Failure of the Open Access Residence Hall Library," 372–380.

18. Oltmanns and Schuh. "Purposes and Uses of Residence Hall Libraries," 172–177.

19. Fischler, "An Analysis of the Use of the Undergraduate Halls of Residence Libraries at Indiana University," 1.

20. Flynn, "There's No Place Like Home," 2.

21. Ibid.

22. Fischler, "An Analysis of the Use of the Undergraduate Halls of Residence Libraries at Indiana University," 2.

23. HRL Archives, "Halls of Residence Libraries Committee Report," Bloomington: Indiana University, Bloomington, 1941.

24. Fischler, "An Analysis of the Use of the Undergraduate Halls of Residence Libraries at Indiana University," 2.

25. Flynn, "There's No Place Like Home," 3.

26. HRL Archives, "Halls of Residence Libraries Committee Report."

27. Gerald H. Doty, "Letter to Robert Irrmann," Bloomington: Indiana University HRL Archives, 1945.

28. Flynn, "There's No Place Like Home," 5.

29. Ibid., 7.

30. Ibid.

31. Ibid., 8.

32. Ibid., 9.

33. Rebecca Smith, "Indiana University Halls of Residence Libraries Records, 1940–2001, Bulk 1950–1970." *Indiana University Archives*, accessed February 10, 2014, http://webapp1.dlib.indiana.edu/findingaids/view?doc.view=entire_text&docId=InU-Ar-VAC0939.

34. Flynn, "There's No Place Like Home," 4.

35. Fischler, "An Analysis of the Use of the Undergraduate Halls of Residence Libraries at Indiana University," 2.

36. Oltmanns and Schuh. "Purposes and Uses of Residence Hall Libraries," 172–177.

37. Ibid., 176.

38. Shawn Wilson, email message to author, February 18, 2014.

39. Pauline Dewan, "Why Your Academic Library Needs a Popular Reading Collection Now More Than Ever," *College & Undergraduate Libraries* 17, no. 1 (2010): 44–64.

40. Phyllis Rudin, "No Fixed Address: The Evolution of Outreach Library Services on University Campuses," *Reference Librarian* 49, no. 1 (2008): 55–75.

41. Catherine Fraser Riehle and Michael C. Witt. "Librarians in the Hall: Instructional Outreach in Campus Residences," *College & Undergraduate Libraries* 16, no. 2/3 (2009): 107–121.

42. Molly Strothmann and Karen Antell, "The Live-In Librarian: Developing Library Outreach to University Residence Halls," *Reference & User Services Quarterly* 50, no. 1 (Fall 2010): 48–58.

43. Dewan, "Why Your Academic Library Needs a Popular Reading Collection Now More Than Ever," 44–64.

44. Tom Kirk, "What Has Happened to Browsing Collections in Academic Libraries?" *Library Issues* 30, no. 5 (2011), 2.

45. Julie Elliott, "Academic Libraries and Extracurricular Reading Promotion," *Reference & User Services Quarterly* 46, no. 3 (2007), 39.

46. Anne Salter and Judith Brook, "Are We Becoming an Aliterate Society? The Demand for Recreational Reading among Undergraduates at Two Universities," *College & Undergraduate Libraries* 14, no. 3 (2007): 27–43.

47. Ibid.

48. Julie Elliott, "Barriers to Extracurricular Reading Promotion in Academic Libraries," *Reference & User Services Quarterly* 48, no. 4 (2009): 340–346.

49. Frank N. Jones, "The Libraries of the Harvard Houses." *Harvard Library Bulletin* 2 (Autumn 1948), 362.

8

VIRTUAL READERS' ADVISORY

Elizabeth Brookbank

As Anwyll and Chawner point out in their recent article about using online tools for readers' advisory, "In this digital information age, it is increasingly important . . . to adopt new technologies to deliver services such as [readers' advisory] to reach users who have become accustomed to interacting with other people through digital channels."[1] Thus, the motivation for engaging in virtual readers' advisory stems from the same user-centered model that many library services are adopting: it is about going where our patrons are—proactively seeking out our audience instead of waiting for them to come to us.

Practically, this means that if there is a segment of the library's patron community that interacts with the library through a blog, Facebook, or Twitter, that is where the library should engage with them when attempting to offer a service like readers' advisory. A library does not have to give up the idea of engaging patrons in in-person activities; it should simply attempt to communicate with patrons on their terms. These same patrons may also come to the library in person, and indeed it is my hope, and the hope of Slow Books, that some of the strategies discussed in this chapter will lead to more college students using the physical academic library buildings for reading-related activities. What this does *not* mean for libraries, however, is that they should start a blog, website, social media profile, and so on solely to do readers' advisory. These online tools—and the decision about whether to engage in them—should be part of a larger conversation about a library's overall strategy regarding promotion, communication, and public services.[2] Therefore, the libraries that will most benefit from the ideas and strategies in this chapter are (1) those that already have a website, blog, or social media profile that they use to communicate with patrons and (2) those that have been convinced by the first part of this book to offer readers' advisory services as a means of sparking a Slow Books movement on their campuses or in their community.

A RATIONALE FOR ONLINE READERS' ADVISORY

The Pew Research Center has produced several reports in recent years about the use of social media in the United States. In 2011, a survey on "College Students and Technology" found that fully 94–99 percent of college students (percentages vary depending on type of college) use the Internet, and 78–86 percent of these Internet users use social media.[3] In addition, Pew's more recent (2013) report "The Demographics of Social Media Users" found that 83 percent of all Internet users aged 18–29 use social networking sites.[4]

Some of the most popular tools are Facebook, Twitter, Pinterest, Instagram, and Tumblr.[5] Facebook is the most popular, with 67 percent of Internet users using the site.[6] Although recent reports suggest that Facebook is losing popularity with young teens,[7] it is currently the most heavily used social network in the United States.[8] The use of Facebook and other social networking tools is further encouraged by use of mobile devices. As two other 2013 Pew reports reveal, 80 percent of adults aged 18–29 own a smartphone[9] and, of these, 85 percent use them to go online.[10] Furthermore, 50 percent of them go online *mostly* using their phones—rather than their computer.[11]

So, yes, college students are using social media and the Internet, albeit more and more on their smartphones. Even so, this does not necessarily mean that students are on their library's blogs, websites, and social media pages. In a review of several different studies on students' reactions to academic institutions using social media, Phillips found that the reactions of students to their library's presence on social media varied widely, from apathy toward the idea of interacting with the library via social media to openness toward becoming fans of library pages on Facebook.[12] Ultimately, the consensus of these studies is that "each library must know the preferences of its own student community."[13] For this reason, this chapter is not tool- or channel-specific in its recommendations but instead provides ideas and advice for practicing virtual readers' advisory using whatever tools and channels make the most sense in a given library and campus community. Even libraries that opt not to have a presence on social media or a blog are likely to at least have a website and thus can still make use of the advice and ideas offered in this chapter.

In addition to accommodating users' online habits, virtual readers' advisory is in many ways easier to manage than in-person readers' advisory. It is easier for the librarians doing it, easier for the students, and easier for the library as an organization. For instance, in the online environment, the librarian does not have to worry about coming up with a suggestion instantaneously with the person standing right there watching.[14] Virtual activities also accommodate commuter and online students who may not use the physical library or students who are intimidated by the reference desk and do not want to approach a librarian face to face. Finally, it is easier for the whole organization, if it is newly introducing a readers' advisory service, to start online only. This is because virtual readers' advisory is scalable; it allows libraries to test the waters by promoting the service for a limited amount of time, and in a limited number of places, to see what the response is and how able librarians are to respond to the demand.[15] This is especially important for academic librarians since readers' advisory is unlikely to be in their job descriptions, and any time devoted to it will need to fit in and around the edges.[16]

Beyond these reasons, providing readers' advisory services online fits with the ethos of readers' advisory. Long-time readers' advisory expert Barry Trott maintains that virtual readers' advisory builds "a community of readers"[17] that librarians can "support . . . by helping them locate stories that affirm and support their lives."[18] On the one hand, as discussed in the first chapter of this book, the distractions of the Internet are the very distractions that can hinder slow reading in our daily lives and in the lives of our students. On the other hand, because social networks are a community and a conversation that college students are already a part of, it behooves us to leverage this community to encourage slow reading. If we are truly committed to creating a culture of reading on our campuses, this should not be the *only way* we do it since at some point we want students to put down their smartphones and pick up a book—or at least navigate to their Kindle app. Virtual readers' advisory is, however, a start.

CURRENT LEADERS IN VIRTUAL READERS' ADVISORY

There are many different ways that online tools are being used to promote reading in both public and academic libraries. Virginia Commonwealth University (VCU) Libraries and Gettysburg College's Musselman Library both maintain blogs focused on books and reading, called *Book reMarks*[19] and *Next Page*[20] respectively. These academic libraries use their blogs to review and recommend books to their campus communities, and both integrate the blog with their library catalogs so that the reviewed books can be easily located and checked out. Musselman Library's catalog itself serves as a readers' advisory tool in that the record for the individual book, which is linked to from the blog post, displays similar items and allows the user to virtually browse the shelf around the featured book. VCU's*Book reMarks* is used as a free resource for book suggestions by the "reference desk staff . . . when answering readers' advisory questions."[21] The world of public libraries offers many additional examples of effective and delightful readers' advisory blogs that an academic library could draw inspiration from, including Seattle Public's *Shelf Talk*,[22] Williamsburg Regional's *Blogging for a Good Book*,[23] and Lawrence Public's *In the Spotlight*.[24]

Many public libraries have started offering "form-based" readers' advisory, which involves posting a form to their website where readers can submit their reading preferences and get reading suggestions back from the librarians.[25] These forms vary widely in length and complexity, ranging from the robust Reader Profile Form that is part of Williamsburg Regional Library's Looking for a Good Book program[26] and the Reader Form that is part of Downers Grove Public Library's I'm in the Mood to Read program[27] to short and simple forms such as those maintained by the London Public Library[28] and the Seattle Public Library as part of their Your Next 5 program.[29]

Social media, mainly Facebook and Twitter, is the other main set of tools used by libraries to both promote reading and to provide readers' advisory services. A study in 2011 found that 13 percent of Facebook messages posted by academic libraries "encouraged reading" in some way.[30] A review of selected academic library Facebook fan pages and Twitter feeds revealed that the most common way for academic libraries to use Facebook and Twitter is to encourage reading by promoting their recreational collections generally, what Newman calls "static" readers' advisory services.[31] UCLA's Powell Library, for instance, has promoted its recreational reading collection with Facebook status updates, links to the collection, pictures of the room the collection is in, and even a short video on Twitter promoting its collection of graphic novels.[32] DePauw University Libraries recently promoted its recreational reading collection by allowing the campus community to vote on what new magazine titles would be added to the collection.[33] Santa Rosa Junior College has instituted #NewTitleTuesday on Facebook and Twitter, in which they promote new individual books that have recently been added to the Doyle Library Leisure Reading collection.[34]

Potomac State College of WVU's Mary F. Shipper Library uses Facebook to promote its PSC Book Lovers book club. In doing so, it also promotes the recreational reading collection and encourages students to read for pleasure.[35] On the main fan page, the library posts reminders about the book club meetings and about the book being read, and it maintains a separate Facebook group for the club itself to talk about the books between their twice a semester face-to-face meetings.[36] The aforementioned Musselman Library posts on Facebook and Twitter about each new entry on its *Next Page* blog.[37] It also uses both Facebook and Twitter to promote the library's annual Summer Reading booklet, "You Gotta Read This,"[38] which is a list that includes book suggestions from "faculty, staff, and administrators . . . to inspire [their] campus community to take time in the summer to sit back, relax, and read."[39]

Another, more direct, way that libraries have used social media in promoting reading is by conducting readers' advisory "interviews" with patrons/students within a social network itself—a readers' advisory service that Newman calls "dynamic" (as opposed to "static").[40] In these interactions, patrons tell librarians over social media about their reading preferences and/or books they have liked in the past, and—using that same social media channel—librarians then give them suggestions for other books they might like.[41] This dynamic, interactive service works particularly well via social media, given the real-time nature of this channel and the fact that many people use social media on the go with their mobile devices. Public libraries, as is the case in most readers' advisory activities, are the leaders in this form of readers' advisory.

Multnomah County Library (MCL) and Seattle Public Library (SPL) are two libraries that have conducted "live" readers' advisory days via Facebook and Twitter. I was lucky enough to participate in one during my graduate school internship with SPL. When someone posts/tweets the names of books they have enjoyed during that day, the library replies within a short period of time with suggestions via the same social media channel to which the reader posted (i.e., someone who posts on the SPL or MCL Facebook page will get a reply to that comment on Facebook; someone who tweets will receive a reply tweet).[42] This tactic, which has been greeted enthusiastically by patrons,[43] seems to be a good mix of both worlds—patrons and librarians enjoy both the ease and the distance that come from interacting online as well as the satisfying immediacy of an almost-in-person interaction.

This type of direct readers' advisory is far less common in academic libraries, but it is a tactic that libraries with popular reading collections and interest in promoting a culture of reading should explore. Not only is it a more lively and interactive form of readers' advisory but it also helps develop students' information literacy skills. As discussed elsewhere in this volume, by asking students about their reading preferences and giving them ideas about how and where to find books that fit those reading preferences, librarians give students practice identifying their own information needs and effectively accessing what they need and want when it comes to their own recreational reading.[44]

Academic libraries are also using social reading websites to encourage recreational reading. Gustavus Adolphus College's Folke Bernadotte Memorial Library maintains a LibraryThing.com account where librarians, faculty, and staff add, rate, and review books.[45] Another social reading website that libraries both public and academic are using is Goodreads.com. For example, Albion College's Stockwell-Mudd Library has a Goodreads profile that it promotes via its website, inviting students to join in discussions about books—an online book club of sorts.[46] On its Goodreads profile, the library adds books and reviews to the site's three categories: Read, Currently Reading, and To Read.[47]

As is clear from all these examples, there are many, many different ways a library could engage in readers' advisory services online. Any such program can and should be customized to fit the specific library, staff, time available, and interests of the students. A library that has a recreational reading collection and would like to begin promoting the collection online and/or providing virtual readers' advisory services will find the following recommendations useful. This list is certainly not exhaustive given the fact that virtual readers' advisory is a new and evolving area, particularly for academic libraries.

RECOMMENDATIONS

Scale promotion—start small. It is not necessary (or advisable!) to try to engage in all the online channels and tactics mentioned in this chapter all at once. The key to beginning a program like this is to start small and then scale up if the initial efforts are successful, staff is interested, and time is available. A library can control how much time and effort these activities take by selectively promoting them, for instance, promoting the service on Facebook but not on the library's homepage (or vice-versa) or by promoting services during a dedicated week or specific day.

Time promotions strategically. Part of customizing virtual readers' advisory activities to fit a library's specific needs and that of its students is thinking about the time of day/week/year that makes the most sense. As Fister found in her study of student attitudes toward recreational reading, "lack of time to read for pleasure, whether because of homework, a desire to socialize, or a decision to spend time in other ways, is the primary constraint."[48] Because of this (real or perceived) lack of time during the school year, Fister suggests focusing readers' advisory activities around breaks in the academic year when students ostensibly have more free time.[49] Consider the schedule and rhythm of your campus when planning readers' advisory promotions and activities so that students are more receptive to the idea of reading (i.e., when they are likely to have more free time).

Keep online best practices in mind. There are not many articles or books that talk specifically about academic libraries engaging in readers' advisory activities online, but there are a good many with advice about how libraries should use social media in general. This type of advice is as well applied to virtual readers' advisory as it is to any other type of social media activity. For instance, it is important for a librarian to answer the question, "What's in it for the student?" when drafting social media posts.[50] Why should students want their campus librarian to suggest a book for them? Why now? Why is a librarian's suggestion better than one they would get elsewhere? Will it be easy for students to access the book(s) suggested? How can they access them? Thinking about questions such as these while drafting readers' advisory promotions will lead to more success overall, as will applying other social media best practices such as making posts actionable by always providing a link,[51] getting to the point in 80 characters or fewer (even if you have 140), and avoiding being bossy or overly excited.[52]

Choose the channel wisely. A good place to begin is with promoting the recreational reading collection via whatever online channels the library already has. If this means simply posting an update or form on the library website, that works. If the library already has a Facebook page, start there. Different channels mean different levels of exposure. For some libraries, the homepage of their website might be the most trafficked and popular part of their online presence. For other libraries, the most popular online space might be the library's Facebook page or Twitter feed. Again, the best channel(s) will depend on the library, staff interest, and the amount of time one can commit. In any case, the level of exposure inherent in promoting readers' advisory services via certain online channels is something that should be considered from the outset.

If promoting via the library's website ...

The most interactive type of website promotion for readers' advisory is the form. As discussed earlier, a form for readers' advisory can take many shapes and can be as complex or as simple as desired. The key is that the reader is able to enter some piece of information about her reading preferences (whether a single title or genre, or an entire reader profile), along with her contact information for a librarian to respond to her with suggestions.[53] The most public and heavily trafficked place to post such a form is likely the homepage of the library's website. But depending on how ready the library is to expand its online readers' advisory presence, the form could also be posted on a page dedicated to reading or readers' advisory located on another, less visible, part of the website.

The Folke Bernadotte Memorial Library does not have a form, but it does have such a dedicated page on its website called Looking for Something to Read? On this page, the library promotes its LibraryThing account and links to other readers' advisory resources, both free and restricted to its students.[54] This type of page, where all a library's readers' advisory and book suggestion resources are collected in one place, is a great idea and much more effective from a user interface perspective than having these resources scattered throughout the library's website.

If promoting via a blog ...

A blog is probably the most labor intensive method for promoting a recreational reading collection and engaging in readers' advisory services. This is simply because it requires more content than a post on social media or a form on a website. Creating a blog from scratch is a large undertaking and one that should not be decided upon lightly. If the library already has a blog that is regularly maintained by assigned staff, however, adding a readers' advisory component could be a great fit.

Obviously, the more context given for each book, in the form of an annotation and/or recommendation, the richer the readers' advisory experience will be for the reader. But writing book annotations and reviews is time consuming, especially if one is new to it or has not done it since library school. Hollands suggests keeping all the annotations written for readers' advisory purposes in a central location that is accessible to everyone and will reliably be around for years to come (e.g., the library intranet, a shared drive). This way, librarians can reuse annotations or at least have a place to start when conducting readers' advisory.[55] This practice will be especially useful for academic librarians who are making suggestions based on a small recreational reading collection; gathering annotations that can be used over and over will save them time.

For ideas and good examples of readers' advisory blog posts, one does not have to look far. There are many public libraries that maintain very good blogs, a few of which I mentioned already. There are also scores of non-library–related book blogs such as *Book Riot, Books on the Nightstand, Book Club Girl, Bookslut, 101 Books*—the list could go on and on.

If promoting via social media . . .

All of the considerations that have already been discussed also apply (in some cases, they apply even more) to social media promotion. Think about timing, maintain best practices, and start small. Remember, half of students are likely reading these promotions on their smartphones,[56] making it even more important to keep posts short and to the point. Ideally, readers' advisory activities would be worked into an existing schedule of posts/tweets/updates for whatever social media channel the library already uses. If promoting the recreational reading collection for the first time, or if promoting a collection that is new, start by simply talking about it so that students are made aware that nonacademic leisure books exist in the library. These types of general promotional posts include pictures of the collection, directions to its location, announcements when new books are added to the collection, or facts and statistics about the collection (types of genres, number of books, number of new books, etc.). Then move on to promoting individual books or genres by posting about individual titles that might be of interest to the audience, promoting new books in a certain genre, or promoting popular books that have been consistently checked out for some time but that are currently available. These posts about individual books will be made better, and more appealing, if they include a short annotation summarizing what the book is about and what type of reader it would appeal to. If the collection is big enough, promote one or two "read-alikes" so that there are other options when someone checks out the originally suggested title. This type of promotion is fairly unidirectional (unless the library has a very active audience that comments on/replies to announcement-like posts) and therefore requires only someone to draft the content of the post and potentially the annotation. Even though these posts are short, it takes a good amount time to craft updates that are clever, concise, and engaging—as all good social media posts should be—so plan accordingly.

Once you are comfortable with these one-way posts, consider engaging in some interactive, direct readers' advisory over social media. This type of readers' advisory, wherein participation is solicited from readers in exchange for reading suggestions, requires more preparation. The posts advertising the readers' advisory services over Facebook or Twitter need to be drafted ahead of time. They should be short and clever, and should ask no more of the audience than to fill out a short form linked in the post or comment with a book title that they have enjoyed in the past. Once the posts are up, someone has to be ready to actually make suggestions—and to make them quickly. The rule of thumb I learned from working with the seasoned readers' advisors at

SPL is to reply within 30 minutes. To reply this quickly, it is a good idea to have some readers' advisory tools at the ready. Try having a browser window with several tabs open to quickly switch between, including Facebook and/or Twitter, the library catalog, a reading site like LibraryThing or Goodreads, a couple of free online readers' advisory websites (many of which are mentioned in Pauline Dewan's chapter in this book), and a blank tab for quick searches. I also keep a catalog search open that pulls up all of the books in our recreational reading collection, and I have several print readers' advisory texts close at hand, just in case.

When responding to someone's comment, it is a good idea to offer more than one suggestion in case the first one falls flat. Since virtual interactions obviously limit the advisor's ability to gauge her patron's reaction (for instance, his or her facial cues), offering more than one suggestion is a good way to take off the pressure. Just remember that Twitter posts are short, so either be brief or reply multiple times to the same person. Also keep in mind that the combination of giving students carte blanche to ask for reading suggestions and having the tacit imperative to reply quickly means that this type of readers' advisory activity can be very time consuming. For this reason, depending on how active the library's social media audience is, it may be a good idea to set time limits on the offer (e.g., "Get reading suggestions if you comment today/within the next hour").

Another readers' advisory activity that could be conducted over social media that is less immediate than direct readers' advisory, but potentially more time consuming, is an online book club. Readers' advisors could use this platform both to promote and facilitate an in-person book club, like the Mary F. Shipper Library, or to conduct a book club entirely online. For the online-only iteration, participants read one book during a set period of time, on their own time (the same as an in-person book club). But instead of meeting in person at regular intervals to discuss the book, the conversation is ongoing via Twitter (or Facebook; either channel would work). As with any book club, an online book club requires some moderation to ensure that the conversation keeps going and is a rich one, that members respect one another, and that no one spoils the book for anyone else. For inspiration and ideas, the well-known Twitter book club @1book140 is a good example.[57]

If promoting via social reading websites . . .

Focusing readers' advisory activities within these websites does run the risk of reaching fewer people since the audience will be limited largely to those who already use these sites (i.e., people who are already readers). LibraryThing and Goodreads have large user populations, but they are not nearly as ubiquitous as social networks like Facebook and Twitter. If the library already has a profile within one of these social reading communities, however, it can certainly be used for readers' advisory and for promoting a culture of reading.

All social reading websites allow users to add books into "collections," and users can follow one another to receive updates when books are added to collections or moved from one collection to another. A library could use these features as a mechanism to suggest certain books or announce when new books are added to their physical or virtual collection. Users can add reviews to books in their collections, which a library could use to annotate and suggest a book to certain types of readers. Goodreads offers the Reading Now designation that allows a user to track his progress through a book and could be used to create a book club within the site. To run such a book club, all the participants would follow the moderator, and each time they began a new book, the moderator would designate it as the book she is Reading Now. She could then update her progress through the book according to where the club is in its reading, and participants could use the comments feature for discussion.[58] Goodreads and Shelfari also allow users to embed "shelves" of books from the site within another website. So, a library could pull content from one of these sites into its main website, making the suggested books much more visible.

MEASURING SUCCESS

Measuring the success of virtual readers' advisory activities should be both a quantitative and a qualitative endeavor, especially since relationships are at the heart of readers' advisory, and personal interactions and successful connections are not easily captured by numbers. Quantitative assessment is still important, though, since it is important to demonstrate that readers' advisory services are making a worthwhile impact and how this impact grows and changes over time. Tracking quantitative data is fairly simple in many of the channels discussed. If anything, there is an overwhelming amount of data available, making it imperative to decide which numbers are important to the library and why, and then tracking those numbers consistently. If possible, capture these statistics before, during, and after running promotions.

The specifics of each channel are different, and each library should track whichever numbers are applicable and relevant to its needs. Overall, however, the important things to know are (1) how many people see the updates and promotions (e.g., the number of page views, followers, fans), (2) how many people interact with these promotions (e.g., comments, replies, retweets, shares, likes), and (3) the content of those interactions so that the library knows what people are actually saying about these services. Remember that we are, ideally, pushing students toward real books (either physical or virtual) that are in our libraries. Therefore, it would behoove the library to track the circulation statistics, including holds/reserves, if possible and applicable, to ascertain whether virtual promotion has had any impact on the real-world actions of students.[59] Finally, it is important to consider how to keep track of readers' advisory questions (both virtual and in person) in relation to other question tracking so that these questions can be reviewed and tracked separately, especially if readers' advisory is a new service and the library is tracking it closely.[60]

CONCLUSION

Although the virtual activities described in this chapter would likely make up just a small part of a library's readers' advisory program, they are an important component in reaching students who may not use the physical library or who may be intimidated by the reference desk. They are also a vital part of encouraging a culture of reading on any campus. Again, college students are among the heaviest users of these tools. And, especially given that social media is a more casual forum, students may feel more in their element and potentially more open to participating in a readers' advisory exchange. This casual and social environment can also be a place for a library to show its personality and make itself more accessible to its students. It is important to scale virtual readers' advisory activities, especially at first, to fit the needs of the specific library, the librarians doing the work, and campus and students' schedule. Consider the timing and level of promotion carefully to encourage reading at a time when students' minds are open to it, as opposed to adding to an already stressful academic year.

Any virtual readers' advisory program, as is the case with all virtual activities that libraries engage in, should be a constantly evolving effort that adapts not only to the specific campus community but also to the always-changing technology. Today, Facebook is still the most popular social network, but there is some indication that is changing, and further, it is now more difficult than ever to reach a library's Facebook fans without paying for promotion.[61] At some point in the future, it might make more sense to take the library's efforts to Instagram[62] or to some other social network not yet invented. Similarly, it might soon be more important for the library to have a mobile phone app than a website, in which case readers' advisory options could be built in. The key for academic libraries that want to engage in virtual readers' advisory services is to integrate them into their current online presence· and to adapt them however that presence changes or evolves.

NOTES

1. Rebecca Anwyll and Brenda Chawner, "Social Media and Readers' Advisory: A Win-Win Combination?" *Reference & User Services Quarterly* 53, no. 1 (2013): 18.

2. There are many books and articles with more information and advice about making these types of decisions, and one of my recently published favorites is Laura Soloman, *The Librarian's Nitty-Gritty Guide to Social Media* (Chicago: ALA Editions, 2013).

3. Aaron Smith, Lee Rainie, and Kathryn Zickuhr, "College Students and Technology," Pew Internet, Pew Research Center, last modified July 19, 2011, accessed December 19, 2013, http://www.pewinternet.org/2011/07/19/college-students-and-technology/.

4. Maeve Duggan and Joanna Brenner, *The Demographics of Social Media Users, 2012* (Washington, D.C.: Pew Research Center's Internet & American Life Project, 2013), 3, accessed December 19, 2013, http://www.pewinternet.org/files/old-media//Files/Reports/2013/PIP_SocialMediaUsers.pdf.

5. Ibid, 2.

6. Ibid.

7. Julianne Pepitone, "Facebook Admits Young Teens Are Losing Interest in the Site," website of *CNN Money*, last modified October 31, 2013, accessed December 19, 2013, http://money.cnn.com/2013/10/30/technology/social/facebook-earnings/; Ryan Tate, "Facebook Swears It's Cool Among Teens—Really," website of *Wired*, last modified November 11, 2013, accessed December 19, 2013, http://www.wired.com/business/2013/11/facebook-teens/; Verne Kopytoff, "'My Mom's on Facebook': Teens Unfriending Network," *Al Jazeera America*, last modified November 18, 2013, accessed December 19, 2013, http://america.aljazeera.com/articles/2013/11/18/-my-mom-s-on-facebookteensincreasinglyunfriendingthesocialnetwor.html.

8. Lee Rainie, Aaron Smith, and Maeve Duggan, *Coming and Going on Facebook* (Pew Internet, Pew Research Center, 2013), 2, accessed December 19, 2013, http://pewinternet.org/Reports/2013/Coming-and-going-on-facebook.aspx.

9. Joanna Brenner, "Pew Internet: Mobile," Pew Internet, Pew Research Center, last modified September 18, 2013, accessed February 26, 2014, http://fe01.pewinternet.org/Commentary/2012/February/Pew-Internet-Mobile.aspx.

10. Maeve Duggan and Aaron Smith, *Cell Internet Use 2013* (Washington, D.C.: Pew Research Center's Internet & American Life Project, 2013), 5, accessed December 19, 2013, http://www.pewinternet.org/files/old-media//Files/Reports/2013/PIP_CellInternetUse2013.pdf.

11. Ibid., 8.

12. Nancy Kim Phillips, "Academic Library Use of Facebook: Building Relationships with Students," *Journal of Academic Librarianship* 37, no. 6 (2011): 513.

13. Ibid.

14. Neal Wyatt, "Take the RA Talk Online," *Library Journal* 133, no. 3 (2008): 32.

15. Barry Trott, "Advising Readers Online: A Look at Internet-Based Reading Recommendation Services," *Reference & User Services Quarterly* 44, no. 3 (2005): 214.

16. Neil Hollands, "Improving the Model for Interactive Readers' Advisory Service," *Reference & User Services Quarterly* 45, no. 3 (2006): 210.

17. Barry Trott, "Building on a Firm Foundation: Readers' Advisory over the Next Twenty-Five Years," *Reference & User Services Quarterly* 48, no. 2 (2008): 134.

18. Trott, "Advising Readers Online," 211.

19. "Book reMarks," VCU Libraries, last modified July 8, 2013, accessed February 26, 2014, http://wp.vcu.edu/book-remarks/.

20. "Next Page," Musselman Library, Gettysburg College, last modified December 4, 2013, accessed November 15, 2013, http://nextpagegettysburg.blogspot.com/.

21. Bosman, Glover, and Prince, "Growing Adult Readers," 51.

22. "Shelf Talk," Seattle Public Library, last modified December 30, 2013, accessed October 18, 2013, http://shelftalk.spl.org/.

23. "Blogging for a Good Book," Williamsburg Regional Library, last modified December 30, 2013, accessed October 18, 2013, http://bfgb.wordpress.com/.

24. "In the Spotlight," Lawrence Public Library, last modified December 26, 2013, accessed December 16, 2013, http://www.lawrence.lib.ks.us/category/in-the-spotlight/.

25. David Wright, "What Form-Based Readers' Advisory Can Do for You," *Alki* 27, no. 3 (2011): 9.

26. "Looking for a Good Book," Williamsburg Regional Library, last modified December 30, 2013, accessed October 11, 2013, http://www.wrl.org/books-and-reading/adults/looking-good-book.

27. "I'm In the Mood to Read," Downers Grove Public Library, last modified October 25, 2013, accessed December 16, 2013, http://www.downersgrovelibrary.org/reader_form.php.

28. "Readers' Advisory," London Public Library, last modified April 2, 2012, accessed December 16, 2013, http://www.london.lib.oh.us/advisory.

29. "Your Next 5 Books," The Seattle Public Library, last modified December 19, 2013, accessed October 11, 2013, https://www.spl.org/using-the-library/get-help/your-next-5-books.

30. Phillips, "Academic Library Use of Facebook," 516.

31. Bobbi Newman, "Taking Readers' Advisory Online," in *Readers' Advisory Handbook*, ed. Jessica E. Moyer and Kaite Mediatore Stover (Chicago: ALA Editions, 2010), 113.

32. UCLA Powell Library's Facebook page, December 15, 2011, accessed December 19, 2013, https://www.facebook.com/UCLA.Powell.Library/posts/289993121037698; Ibid, July 17, 2012, https://www.facebook.com/photo.php?fbid=408712895832386&set=a.262285503808460.57483.144156655621346&type=1; Ibid, March 22, 2012, https://www.facebook.com/photo.php?fbid=345459175491092&set=a.262285503808460.57483.144156655621346&type=1; UCLA Powell Library's Twitter feed, March 8, 2013, accessed December 29, 2013, https://twitter.com/UCLA_Powell/status/310096718966423552.

33. DePauw University Libraries' Facebook page, September 16, 2013, accessed December 9, 2013, https://www.facebook.com/DePauwLibraries/posts/10151720171404051.

34. Santa Rosa Junior College Library's Facebook page, November 26, 2013, accessed December 9, 2013, https://www.facebook.com/photo.php?fbid=10152097666042160&set=a.466085217159.251263.13979307159&type=1; SRJC Libraries' Twitter feed, December 17, 2013, accessed December 29, 2013, https://twitter.com/srjclibrary/status/413157110462316544.

35. Potomac State College of WVU, Mary F. Shipper Library's Facebook page, September 22, 2013, accessed December 9, 2013, https://www.facebook.com/permalink.php?story_fbid=723577317659539&id=128346157182661.

36. PSC Book Lovers Facebook group, last modified December 14, 2013, accessed December 9, 2013, https://www.facebook.com/groups/PSCBookLovers/.

37. Musselman Library's Facebook page, December 4, 2013, accessed December 9, 2013, https://www.facebook.com/MusselmanLibrary/posts/669137543116498; Musselman Library's Twitter feed, December 11, 2013, accessed December 29, 2013, https://twitter.com/GburgColLibrary/status/410834449753202688.

38. Musselman Library's Twitter feed, May 8, 2013, accessed December 29, 2013, https://twitter.com/GburgColLibrary/status/332229686660825089; Musselman Library's

Facebook page, June 7, 2013, accessed December 9, 2013, https://www.facebook.com/MusselmanLibrary/posts/581795735184013.

39. "You've Gotta Read (or Watch) This!" *MussGettInfo!* (blog), May 7, 2012, accessed November 15, 2013, http://musselmanlibrary.blogspot.com/2012/05/youve-gotta-read-or-watch-this.html.

40. Newman, "Taking Readers' Advisory Online," 113.

41. Alison Kastner, "Facebook RA," *Library Journal* 136, no. 8 (2011): 24; Seattle Library's Twitter feed, June 4, 2013, accessed December 29, 2013, https://twitter.com/SPLBuzz/status/341985505380007936.

42. The Seattle Public Library's Facebook page, June 4, 2013, accessed December 29, 2013, https://www.facebook.com/SeattlePublicLibrary/posts/10151410731996339; Seattle Library's Twitter feed, June 4, 2013, accessed December 29, 2013, https://twitter.com/SPLBuzz/status/342040631654363136.

43. The Seattle Public Library's Facebook page, June 4, 2013, accessed December 29, 2013, https://www.facebook.com/SeattlePublicLibrary/posts/10151410731996339; Kastner, "Facebook RA," 24; Multnomah County Library's Facebook page, December 10, 2013, accessed December 29, 2013, https://www.facebook.com/photo.php?fbid=10152297944824881&set=a.95676234880.76523.90704854880&type=1; Seattle Library's Twitter feed, June 4, 2013, accessed December 29, 2013, https://twitter.com/SPLBuzz/status/342104827284832256.

44. "Information Literacy Competency Standards for Higher Education," Association of College and Research Libraries (ACRL), last modified January 18, 2000, accessed October 2, 2013, http://www.ala.org/acrl/standards/informationliteracycompetency.

45. "Your Books," Folke Bernadotte Memorial Library, Gustavus Adolphus College, last modified March 13, 2013, accessed October 11, 2013, http://www.librarything.com/catalog/FolkeB; "FolkeB's reviews," Folke Bernadotte Memorial Library, Gustavus Adolphus College, last modified March 13, 2013, accessed October 11, 2013, http://www.librarything.com/profile_reviews.php?view=FolkeB.

46. "New Goodreads Books," Stockwell-Mudd Library, Albion College, last modified June 24, 2012, accessed November 27, 2013, http://campus.albion.edu/library/2012/03/new-goodreads-books; "Search Results: Goodreads" Stockwell-Mudd Library," Stockwell-Mudd Library, *Albion College*, last modified September 20, 2013, accessed November 27, 2013, http://campus.albion.edu/library/?s=Goodreads.

47. "Albion College's Profile," Stockwell-Mudd Library, Albion College, last modified July 29, 2013, accessed October 4, 2013, http://www.goodreads.com/user/show/5840798-albion-college.

48. Gilbert and Fister, "Reading, Risk, and Reality," 482.

49. Ibid, 489.

50. Solomon, *The Librarian's Nitty-Gritty Guide to Social Media*, 77

51. Anwyll and Chawner, "Social Media and Readers' Advisory," 19.

52. Solomon, *The Librarian's Nitty-Gritty Guide to Social Media*, 77–79.

53. Wright, "Form-Based Readers' Advisory," 9–10.

54. "Looking for Something to Read?" Folke Bernadotte Memorial Library, Gustavus Adolphus College, accessed October 4, 2013, https://gustavus.edu/library/RA.html.

55. Neil Hollands, "Improving the Model for Interactive Readers' Advisory Service," *Reference & User Services Quarterly*, 45, no. 3 (2006): 211.

56. Maeve Duggan and Aaron Smith, *Cell Internet Use 2013*, 5, accessed December 19, 2013, http://pewinternet.org/Reports/2013/Cell-Internet.aspx.

57. "1book140: TheAtlantic.com's Reading Club," *Atlantic.com*, last modified December 30, 2013, accessed January 31, 2014, http://www.theatlantic.com/entertainment/category/1book140/.

58. Paula Dewan, "Reading Matters in the Academic Library: Taking the Lead from Public Libraries," *Reference & User Services Quarterly* 52, no. 4 (2013): 316.

59. Anwyll and Chawner, "Social Media and Readers' Advisory," 20.

60. Trott, "Advising Readers Online," 215.

61. Jen McDonnell, "Facebook's Algorithm Change Just Cut Your Brand's Reach by Half. So Now What?" *Reshift Media.com* (blog), October 15, 2012, http://www.reshiftmedia.com/facebooks-algorithm-change-just-cut-your-brands-reach-by-half-so-now-what/.

62. Danielle Salomon, "Moving on from Facebook," *College & Research Libraries News* 74, no. 8 (2013): 408, http://crln.acrl.org/content/74/8/408.full.pdf+html.

PART III

Beyond the Academic Library: A Lifetime of Slow Books

9

Collaborating with Local High Schools: Your Senior Will Be My First-Year Student

Sarah Fay Philips and Emerson Case

Many high school students spend every waking hour reading emails, tweets, and text messages on their mobile devices. They rapidly respond in small bits of text without taking time to analyze the message or evaluate their own response. These responses are often constructed while the student is simultaneously engaged in face-to-face conversations with other family or friends, studying, or—as most teachers have experienced—while sitting in a classroom. Furthermore, it is not uncommon for students to sleep with their devices so that they can respond to messages 24 hours a day! These "reading" experiences may be embedded in the hourly life of the student, but they do not inspire them to examine their way of thinking about themselves or their world. Although students spend hours a day reading short strings of text, it is uncommon to meet a high school student who has a favorite book or is currently reading a book for pleasure.

Yet, as these students transition to college, their success largely depends on their ability to understand, connect with, and enjoy the experience of reading. Those students who have developed a reading habit before entering college are more prepared to engage in reflection and the deep, critical thinking that a college curriculum requires.

Libraries are uniquely positioned to promote the reading of literature, expose students to both critical reading and pleasure reading, and better prepare these students for college-level reading and research. By bringing the experience of One Book One Community (OBOC) and the First-Year Experience (FYE) to high school students, college and university librarians can introduce them to college culture, helping them adapt to the roles and expectations of the college student. For some students, especially first-generation college students—many of whom attend California State University Bakersfield—this exposure may be the *only* exposure they have to college or the only time they have engaged in community or literary arts activities outside of the classroom. Thus, in reaching an even broader population of young readers, and in building community around reading, such an outreach effort has the potential to further and deepen the impact of the Slow Books movement.

Put another way, if Slow Books is akin to Slow Food, then a literacy outreach program for high school students combining OBOC programming and the FYE curriculum is akin to high school students harvesting vegetables from a community garden, working with peers under the guidance of a chef to create a meal, and then sharing the meal with other members of the larger community. This literacy outreach program encourages students to grapple with the ideas not only in their own minds but in their own communities and with their own families. This experience is not just about making a connection with a book but making a personal connection with the author and other readers. Building this community is a major goal of Slow Books.

At California State University–Bakersfield (CSUB), the authors combined an OBOC Common Reader partnership with elements from our FYE campus program and brought them to a feeder high school. By connecting students with literature and by providing them with opportunities to participate in literacy activities in the community, this literacy outreach program introduced high school students to the relevant skills and experiences that they need to be successful college students and, by extension, lifelong learners.

This chapter is a case study that illustrates how the CSUB Library and FYE program partnered with the Kern County Library and a feeder high school to address student learning outcomes related to multiculturalism, literacy, and college preparation. Through this program, young people connect with books and develop a relationship with Slow Books.

HIGH SCHOOL AND UNIVERSITY LIBRARY PARTNERSHIPS: A BRIEF HISTORY

Traditional partnerships between academic libraries and secondary schools focus on information literacy instruction as the tool for transition from high school to university. High school students are invited to use a college library for an authentic immersive academic research experience. The students are often allowed to use subscription resources that are not available at their secondary schools. Some university libraries extend borrowing privileges for high school students when their research exceeds their high school library holdings. The opportunity is frequently taken advantage of by honors or International Baccalaureate cohorts, high-performing students who are very likely to attend college. But outreach is needed to introduce the role of Slow Reading in lifelong learning to all students.

CALIFORNIA STATE UNIVERSITY–BAKERSFIELD: A BRIEF HISTORY

CSUB is located in Bakersfield, California, a city at the southern end of central California's San Joaquin Valley, an area dominated by the oil and agriculture industries. The university, which opened in 1970, serves a diverse body of 8,500 students, 47 percent of whom are Hispanic, 25 percent Caucasian, 7 percent African American, and 6 percent Asian/Pacific Islander.[1] Despite the fact that the population of Kern County tops 840,000, CSUB is the only four-year school within a hundred miles in any direction.[2]

The motivation to implement the program described in this chapter was predicated on many areas of concern that characterize the Bakersfield and Kern County areas. For example, a 2008 report from the Brookings Institute characterized Bakersfield as the least-educated metropolitan area in the United States.[3] According to this report, only 14.7 percent of the area's adults 25 and older have earned a bachelor's degree, while only 70.2 percent have earned a high school diploma.[4] Other areas of concern also involve Kern County as a whole, which has the lowest college-going rate, at 44.1 percent, and the highest dropout rate, at 16 percent, in the state of California. The college-going rate is particularly acute among the socioeconomically disadvantaged (31.7%) and English learners (11.3%).[5]

This lack of degree attainment puts the students that CSUB was created to serve at a great disadvantage, since they lack a "college-going" role model in their homes who they can emulate. According to the latest statistics available, only 18 percent of CSUB's new students come from homes where a parent has earned a bachelor's degree, while 25 percent come from homes where a parent has no high school degree or GED, and 15 percent come from homes where a parent has not completed an eighth grade education.[6] Also of great concern is the fact that only one quarter of the regularly admitted first-time freshmen entering CSUB place into both college-level English and college-level mathematics; thus, three quarters of the students in their first year require extensive remediation. Rates of required remediation are even greater for minority students.[7]

FIRST-YEAR EXPERIENCE AND THE RUNNER READER: A BRIEF HISTORY

FYE is a national movement in higher education to help students transition into college. Reading experiences organized around the first year are a common element of FYE. Such experiences, like the Runner Reader Common Reader program at CSUB, are designed "to provide a common academic experience for all first-year students and to strengthen the academic atmosphere of the institution from the first day the student arrives on campus."[8] The mission statement of the CSUB FYE program is "to build, nurture and sustain a vibrant educational community at CSUB committed to the academic and personal success of undergraduate students 'in transition.' "[9]

Each year, the Common Read book at CSUB is selected by the CSUB FYE administrators in consultation with college faculty, community interest groups, and local school stakeholders. The books are identified based on how well the book relates to local issues, multiculturalism, and young adult themes. The literature from the FYE field has clearly demonstrated the power of a Common Reader program, as Fidler states, to "influence students' expectations about academic experiences" and to "help students' sense of connectedness to the institution even before they reach campus."[10] Following Fidler, our goals at CSUB were "to initiate students into a community of scholars that includes faculty, student affairs professionals, and other students,"[11] all of whom can help high school students make connections across disciplines and give them a head start in developing college-level reading skills.

Central to the CSUB FYE program is bringing the author of the Common Read to campus for a public talk that all of campus and the community are invited to attend. As Moser found in administering the reading program at Brooklyn College, "For the great majority of our students, the experience of hearing an author read from a work that they have read and discussed in class, of asking questions of the writer, of engaging in discussion with someone who has written and published a work of literature, is something entirely new, a festive initiation into a community of readers and writers of which they are not likely to have imagined themselves as members."[12] Thus, to invite students into the academic and literary community, we thought it essential that they experience an actual interaction with a major writer.

While Common Reader programs are routine practice on many college campuses, we took our program a step further by expanding it into a literacy outreach activity at a feeder high school. It is well known that the transition between high school and college is among the most difficult, and this is especially true for students who lack the academic preparation necessary for college and the college-going model at home or in their community. We found that waiting until a student was enrolled at CSUB to begin the transition to college and develop a love of slow reading was too late. The process needs to start earlier, and combining high school outreach with a Common Read was a natural solution.

ONE BOOK ONE COMMUNITY: A BRIEF HISTORY

With the Runner Reader embedded in CSUB campus curriculum and programming, the decision was made to expand the program to the community by partnering with the public library and the One Book, One Bakersfield,

One Kern (OBOBOK) programming. The Kern County Public Library had been holding OBOC events since 2007, but it was not until partnering with the university that the cultural offerings associated with the selected Slow Book reading became a central part of the community. A valuable outcome of this partnership is the promotion of higher education and Slow Books, both of which are vitally important in a community with a very low rate of college degree attainment and low college-going rates. This partnership has proven to be tremendously successful, with attendance at events increasing as more community members were included.[13]

As an example, the fall 2011 selection, *The Other Wes Moore,* by Wes Moore, served as the Runner Reader at CSUB and the One Book, One Bakersfield, One Kern selection. With donor funds, the CSUB FYE program purchased multiple copies for each of the libraries in the Kern High School District. Community and university campus events included book discussions, town hall meetings, dramatic readings, panel discussions, a local history lecture, a poetry slam, and live theatre. More than 8,000 people participated in community programming throughout the county and at the university campus. Mr. Moore spoke to approximately 1,700 people at the CSUB campus.

SEVEN WAYS TO OUTREACH

The CSUB FYE curriculum is designed to help students gain the skills necessary to bridge the gap from high school to the university and therefore provides an ideal set of resources for outreach with feeder high school students. The common goals of Slow Books and our outreach program are to (1) facilitate reflection and deep critical thinking, (2) expand a student's ability to empathize and develop social consciousness, and (3) improve academic success. Although promoting lifelong learning can be seen as separate from promoting higher education, we work to achieve both aims.[14]

An important part of our outreach is to bring a love of reading Slow Books to high school students through community collaboration. Relationships with individual instructors were initially begun through the long-established writing outreach programs to provide professional development for high school English teachers. Relationships were developed and strengthened through community partnerships like One Book, One Bakersfield, One Kern. Documents such as the "Blueprint for Collaboration"[15] provide general guidance, and our relationships with instructors working at feeder high schools allowed for problem solving and the development of curriculum that best served the students. Feeder high school students felt connected to the college experience because they were reading the same book, attending the same events, hearing lectures from college professors, talking to new college students, and writing essays from the same prompt as college students.

The literacy outreach program that we developed consists of seven major activities. The first four of these activities are held during a regular class session and take place every two weeks during the fall term and are followed by reflection writing assignments. They are designed to acculturate students to the college-going experience, introducing them to faculty, college students, and college-level work. The final three activities, on the other hand, are designed to engage students in the broader community, culminating with the opportunity to hear and meet the author of the Common Read.

1. As the first high school outreach activity, co-author Dr. Emerson Case, the curriculum coordinator for the CSUB FYE program and English professor at CSUB, visits English classes, gives an overview of the foundations of the university system, and leads a discussion on the differences between high school and college culture. Topics include the important distinctions between high school and college, including grading, attendance, and exams, and such issues as freedom versus responsibility and contact with professors. During this initial visit, he distributes copies of the Common Reader to the students. In a reflection paper following the first activity, one high school senior wrote that "Dr. Case's visit was very eye-opening because he really helped us see that college is nothing like high school. He really helped me see that college involves a lot of responsibility and determination."
2. For the second outreach activity, a high school English teacher and adjunct CSUB English composition instructor gives a lecture and leads a discussion on the differences between high school- and college-level writing. The students invariably express surprise at the challenges of college-level writing, with one student reflecting, "The expectations are hard. I feel scared, I feel I'm almost ready. I don't know how well high school has prepared me for college. Now I'm feeling unconfident, but I'm really happy they're coming in to speak with us. It's sort of a reality check. I think it's beneficial for them to come in."
3. For the third outreach activity, students at the feeder high school are given the opportunity to experience a college-level lecture contextualized by the Runner Reader they have been examining in class and through community events. For example, in 2010, Dr. Gabriel Gutiérrez, director of the Center for the Study of the Peoples of the Americas (CESPA) and associate chair and professor in the Department of Chicano/a Studies at California State University–Northridge, who was scheduled to speak at CSUB later that day, came to the feeder high school and gave the students a historical perspective on the Common Reader through his presentation " 'Amanzar': Historical and Cultural Readings of Victor Villaseñor's Educational Journey in *Burro Genious.*" In 2011, Dr. Sheila Lloyd, assistant professor of English at the University of Redlands, who also spoke at CSUB later that day, came to the feeder

high school and gave an interactive and multimedia presentation based on a critical examination of *The Other Wes Moore*. This was the first college-level lecture for the high school students, but it was made relevant because the content was familiar to them from their Slow Reading. Commenting on Dr. Lloyd's talk, one of the students wrote in a reflection paper that "In many ways this lecture was different from a high school lecture. The tone and language & vocab she used was advanced and gave us a little taste of how college professors speak."

4. As the fourth high school outreach activity, three or four of the second-year student mentors from CSUB came to speak to the classes. The mentors led a discussion on the differences between high school and college from a college student's perspective, followed by an interactive question-and-answer session. In a reflection paper on this discussion, a student wrote, "I learned that in college you have more freedom but more responsibilities. I learned that I need to take advantage of the opportunities I have right now and prepare myself for college right now before it's too late."
5. The final three outreach activities focus on involving high school students in community and university campus events that are related to the Common Read. The fifth activity is provided through the partnership with the OBOBOK program. Students are invited and incentivized with extra credit to attend one or more of the programs designed to engage the community in reading the Common Reader. As part of this wider community discussion, one student attended a book discussion at a locally owned bookstore and wrote, "Today I went to Russo's Bookstore for some extra credit. In all honesty, I expected it to be a drag but overall . . . that experience was something I don't regret. It wasn't the Moore part that I liked, it was the talks about life." This reflection clearly demonstrates how a Common Reader builds community and thus furthers the goals of Slow Books.
6. The sixth outreach activity is an essay contest sponsored by the feeder high school and the Kern High School District. Throughout the fall term, high school students discuss the book using the expository writing module developed for the text and then complete the essay assignment for the module. This essay assignment is based on the same prompt used by the FYE students at CSUB, giving students the chance to experience writing at a college level. Judges for the essay contest are CSUB professors. To give the high school students exposure to campus culture, three essay contest winners and their families are invited to campus. The author of the Common Reader and the university president present their awards at a private afternoon reception at the university library. At the reception, the author gives a brief talk that invariably includes a personal description and discussion of the role of libraries and books in the author's personal development.

7. The seventh and final outreach activity, the high point of the program, is the author's campus visit. The event takes place in the evening and includes an hour-long keynote address and question-and-answer session by the author. This is followed by a book signing that often goes late into the night (e.g., author Wes Moore did not finish signing books and greeting students until 11:45 p.m.). The high school students are invited to attend, and those that are in the audience are invariably moved by the experience. For example, one student, writing in a reflection paper for the high school English class, stated, "My experience at the Wes Moore event at CSUB was really fun. I had no idea there were going to be so many people, but I guess that is college. But while Wes Moore was talking I could tell that he tried to relate all his experiences to us in hopes that he could enlighten people of the same background to become a really good citizen and person in life."

CONCLUSION

Academic libraries and local schools mutually benefit from outreach programs that promote literacy, college preparedness, and multicultural sensitivity among students. The involvement of the university with literacy at the high school level is an investment in the future of the community and the university. Academic librarians positioning themselves in a role of leadership when it comes to promoting Slow Reading is natural and beneficial to the profession, the community, and the university.

NOTES

1. "CSUB Facts & Figures," CSUB Facts & Figures, accessed January 29, 2014, http://www.csub.edu/about_csub/facts/index.html.

2. "State and County QuickFacts [Kern County, California]," website of the U.S. Census Bureau, accessed January 29, 2014, http://quickfacts.census.gov/qfd/states/06/06029.html.

3. Alan Berube et al., *The State of Metropolitan America*, (Washington D.C.: Metropolitan Policy Program at Brookings, 2010), http://www.brookings.edu/~/media/research/files/reports/2010/5/09%20metro%20america/metro_america_report.pdf.

4. Jorge Barrientos, "Both Graduation, Dropout Rates down Slightly in Kern," *Bakersfield Californian*, June 27, 2012, http://www.bakersfieldcalifornian.com/local/x1330930603/Both-graduation-dropout-rates-down-slightly-in-Kern.

5. Joanna Lin, "College-Going Rates Vary Widely in California," *California Watch*, October 18, 2011, http://californiawatch.org/dailyreport/college-going-rates-vary-widely-california-13121.

6. Cheryl Holsonbake, "First Generation Analysis, Fall 2010" (presented at the CSUB Institutional Research and Planning Assessment, Bakersfield, California, May 2011).

7. Terry Dunn, "Academic Progress of CSUB's New Students" (California State University Bakersfield, August 2009).

8. L. Patterson, "New Ideas in First-Year Reading Programs from around the Country," *First-Year Experience Newsletter* 143 (2002): 8–9.

9. Sarah Fay Philips and Emerson Case, "Contextualizing Information Literacy Enrichment through a Common Reader in a First-Year Experience Seminar," *College & Undergraduate Libraries* 20, no. 1 (2013): 1–24, doi:10.1080/10691316.2013.761046.

10. Dorothy S Fidler, "Getting Students Involved from the Get-Go: Summer Reading Programs across the Country," *About Campus* 2 (1997): 32.

11. Ibid.

12. Janet Moser, "The Uncommon in Common Reading Programs: The Freshman Reading Program at Brooklyn College," *Currents in Teaching and Learning* 2, no. 2 (Spring 2010): 89–97.

13. Sarah Fay Philips and Emerson Case, "With a Village: Community One Book Partnership Ameliorates College Preparation Deficit," *ACRL 2013* (April 10, 2013): 651–658.

14. John A. Cosgrove, "Promoting Higher Education," *College & Undergraduate Libraries* 8, no. 2 (2001): 17–24, doi:10.1300/J106v08n02_02.

15. AASL/ACRL Task Force on the Educational Role of Libraries, "Blueprint for Collaboration," accessed September 20, 2013, http://www.ala.org/acrl/publications/whitepapers/acrlaaslblueprint.

10

BEYOND COLLEGE: COLLABORATING WITH YOUR PUBLIC LIBRARIAN

Rebecca Malinowski

As a public librarian who hosts a monthly book discussion for adults in their twenties and thirties, I was intrigued by the idea of the Slow Books movement on college campuses, particularly by its potential to engage 20-somethings in book discussions. Meagan Lacy's recent ALA presentation, in which she described her book club at Indiana University–Purdue University Indianapolis,[1] for example, struck me not only as a successful way to engage students but also as an opportunity for her to connect with the public library. From experience, I know that connecting with college-aged adults is difficult for the public library. *Maybe*, I thought, *the public library could help Lacy secure multiple copies of their discussion titles, develop further reading lists, or cross-promote Lacy's discussion in their library or vice versa. Maybe the public library in that community already had a discussion for adults in their twenties and thirties, and the two groups could come together for a joint discussion. What if there were a floating collection of titles curated by library staff to support the Slow Books movement? What if the public library picked up the movement as well, and it became a community-wide initiative?* A lot of maybes and what-ifs.

Thinking more specifically about the goals of the Slow Books movement—connecting readers with books they can savor, teaching them to value their reading time, guiding them as they explore their tastes, and creating a culture of reading—I started to identify mutually beneficial ways that public and academic libraries can work together to support these goals. First, public librarians possess a wealth of readers' advisory experience and expertise that they can share with academic librarians, who may be more focused on reference and instructional services. Second, academic and public librarians can work together to create new program and outreach initiatives that will support the

Slow Books movement by bolstering the role of the library in community members' lives, thereby encouraging lifelong reading. This chapter seeks to present practical options for partnerships, with notes on how to adapt ideas to serve the specific needs of your library.

DEFINING PARTNERSHIP

To say that there are no existing partnerships between academic and public libraries would be an overstatement. But as Kathleen Halverson points out in "Creating and Capitalizing on the Town/Gown Relationship: An Academic Library and a Public Library form a Community Partnership," one-on-one partnerships between college libraries and public libraries are rare.[2] More common are models of coordination and cooperation, as defined by Joan Giescke in her 2012 article, "The Value of Partnerships." Coordination, Giescke writes, "Emphasizes efficiency in working together with a minimal amount of involvement by participants."[3] Cooperation, in contrast, requires more interaction from member organizations as groups "come together to share resources such as space, funds, or time."

More intricate than either coordination or cooperation is true collaboration, or the formation of a partnership. Giescke quotes Michael Schrage's *Shared Minds* in which Schrage defines collaboration as "the process of shared creating: two or more individuals with complementary skills interacting to create a shared understanding that none had previously possessed or could have come to on their own."[4] Given the overlapping mission and goals of most public and academic libraries, paired with the shrinking budgets and increased demands on staff time that many agencies in both fields face, it is surprising that there are not more examples in the literature of partnerships.

EXISTING ACADEMIC-PUBLIC PARTNERSHIPS

Consortial agreements are an example of *cooperation*, as they involve joint goal setting and shared resources, but members retain their independence. There are multitype consortia such as the Southeast Florida Library Information Network (SEFLIN), whose mission reads:

> SEFLIN cultivates cooperation and coordination among libraries of all types, nurtures efficient and effective information resource sharing, advances technological innovation, provides staff development opportunities, and advocates for our libraries and their patrons.

Organizations like SEFLIN focus on large-scale projects like shared purchases, conferences, and job boards.[5] Smaller cooperatives exist, many of which focus on shared catalogs. For example, the Cedar Valley Library Consortium shared catalog comprises collections from community colleges, a four-year university, and public libraries.[6] Another example is the partnership between Keene State College and Keene Public Library in New Hampshire, in which a joint catalog has led to "a real community tie, which brings members of the college and the city of Keene into contact with each other."[7] While these arrangements provide greater access to materials for library users on both ends, there seem to be few efforts to engage in further shared endeavors. One way to push this type of cooperation into the realm of collaboration would be to explore floating collections. While it is a logistically challenging prospect, library users of this kind of multitype partnership could benefit from the diversity of their institutions' collections.

One model of *collaboration* that is being practiced is a joint use space, which we see in San Jose, California. The King Library is co-owned and co-managed by the San Jose Public Library and San Jose State University.[8] The two organizations "married" their libraries, and as a result, they enjoy a larger facility, greater diversity of materials, and longer operating hours than either agency could manage on its own. The support of the mayor and university president was vital to this unique partnership, and the intricacies of their new model make it inaccessible for most other libraries looking to develop multitype partnerships.

There are also examples in the literature of academic and public libraries collaborating on specific events, as did librarians at Miami University (Ohio) for a Japanese cultural festival.[9] In their "Promoting Partnership: Campus and Community Collaboration through Cultural Events," Stacy Brinkman and Frances Weinstein Yates acknowledge that large-scale events such as the cultural festival require more staff time and resources than the university library could allocate on its own.[10] Cultural programs, they write, "are an excellent way to get the library connected with students' extracurricular activities and interests."[11] Single-day programs, whether as extensive as an all-community event like the cultural festival or a smaller-scale program, can open doors to collaboration or take advantage of existing relationships.

Tom Wilding, in "External Partnerships and Academic Libraries," presents public libraries as potential partners for academic libraries looking to "offer the community expanded access to high quality information resources"[12] and says that the cooperating libraries "[add] value to the community's cultural and education life,"[13] though he does not elaborate on what these partnerships might entail. The following sections outline concrete suggestions for possible academic-public partnerships.

PARTNERING IN READERS' ADVISORY

Readers' advisory would be an ideal candidate for such a partnership. According to Connie Van Fleet, obstacles academic librarians face in developing an RA practice include staff and administrators' negative perceptions of popular culture, perceptions that popular fiction is not a part of the library's mission, and lack of education and training in popular fiction.[14] But Pauline Dewan, herself an academic librarian, argues in "Reading Matters in the Academic Library" that recreational reading promotion is a part of the academic library's mission, and furthermore, public librarians are at the forefront of pleasure reading promotion.[15] This latter observation suggests that academic librarians could learn a lot from their public librarian colleagues.

In *Slow Reading in a Hurried Age*, David Mikics writes, "Not all books are for all readers,"[16] which echoes Ranganathan's second and third laws—every reader his book and every book its reader.[17] While Mikics does ask slow readers to "stretch" their taste,[18] he also assures readers, "Your patient struggle with a book should be fun, not tedious. Force-reading is as bad as force-feeding; if you're simply cramming down a book because you think it will be good for you, find something you'll like better instead."[19] Most librarians will acknowledge that this is good advice. But the act of fitting a book to its reader and a reader its book is an art. It takes time for a librarian to develop this skill, let alone the average reader. Especially for college-aged readers who are still exploring and stretching their tastes, maybe even getting their first taste of reading without a syllabus as an adult, selecting a title to read can be overwhelming. Faced with endless possibilities, it is easy to be paralyzed with indecision. A librarian supporting the Slow Books movement, then, should be prepared to advise these readers as they explore the literary world.

One of the most daunting aspects of readers' advisory is, arguably, feeling expected to know enough about every title, author, or genre to help any patron off the cuff. It is easy to feel unprepared, especially in the face of a question as broad as "Can you help me find a good book?" As Pauline Dewan points out in Chapter 3, librarians have many tools to help in the moment. While they are all excellent tools, developing a solid foundation and regularly adding to our knowledge base is key to feeling confident as readers' advisors. This is where partnering with a public librarian can be helpful.

Readers' advisors in public libraries are always building their knowledge base by reading across genres, keeping careful notes, and participating in continuing education and professional development. But where should an academic librarian looking to develop a RA practice start? It may have been years since your last RA class, if you even had the opportunity to take one. Staff time and budgets are tight across the board, and the resources you have to invest in jumpstarting your RA services may be slim. Luckily, there is probably an expert in the subject right around the corner.

Readers' advisory, as we know it today, has been a focus in many public libraries since the 1982 publication of Betty Rosenberg's *Genreflecting*.[20] The RA librarian focused on developing the knowledge and skills needed to help the public find books to read for pleasure, whether popular or literary. Rosenberg's first rule is, "Never apologize for your reading tastes." For over 30 years, nationally known librarians like Joyce Saricks, Neal Wyatt, and

Nancy Pearl as well as librarians working within their communities, have been developing tools to help public librarians develop their RA practices with Rosenberg's first rule in mind.

Collaborating with the public library to train readers' advisors can be mutually beneficial, and there are a number of forms of varying intensity that the partnership could take. In the next sections, I will describe a number of ongoing training and development opportunities that you may find or initiate in your area along with your public librarian, including Genre Boot Camp, a program designed by public librarians to get new readers' advisors up to speed on trends in fiction.

WHERE TO START

The Chicagoland-based Adult Reading Round Table (ARRT) provides tools that can be of use to librarians working to develop their RA practice. Founded in 1984 by a group of public librarians, including Joyce Saricks, the mission of the ARRT is "developing Readers' Advisory skills and promoting reading for pleasure through public libraries in the Chicago metropolitan area."[21] In addition to providing quarterly continuing education programs, ARRT sponsors literary book discussions, hosts in-depth explorations of popular genres called genre studies, and publishes annual bibliographies for its members.

The most extensive of these bibliographies is the *Adult Popular Fiction List*, which is "designed to help library staff evaluate their knowledge of popular fiction for adults."[22] While this list is not designed to offer read-alikes during a patron interaction, it is an efficient way to gauge library staff's familiarity with genres and identify gaps in knowledge, and it is a great place for new readers' advisors to begin.

The list is divided into umbrella categories and genres, with an introduction to each, along with key elements and appeal factors, which leads to a list of living authors currently popular among readers. For example, "Crime Fiction" is listed as an umbrella category, "Mystery" is the genre, and "Amateur Detective" is the subgenre.[23] A grid, listing the names of popular authors that readers' advisors should be aware of, follows these descriptions. Library staff using the tool would work through each list, noting their familiarity with the authors therein by marking one of four options:

R = I've read this author
RA = I've read about this author (reviews, interviews, etc.)
H = I've heard of this author (patron or colleague comments)
NH = I've never heard of this author[24]

Whether preparing to attend a group training or developing an individual learning plan, working through the *Adult Popular Fiction List* can help readers' advisors of all skill levels identify areas of study to target.

GENRE BOOT CAMP

With each release of the Adult Popular Fiction List, ARRT has presented Genre Boot Camp, a single-day conference designed to introduce librarians to the Adult Popular Fiction List and help them get up to speed in key genres. As a member of the ARRT Steering Committee, I was tasked with developing the 2013 Genre Boot Camp with Steering Committee members Nancy McCully (Glenside Public Library) and Karen Toonen (Naperville Public Library). Although the strength of Genre Boot Camp comes from both the number of experts recruited to lead sessions and the number of attendees involved in discussions throughout the day, the format could be scaled back, stretched over a number of shorter sessions, or presented asynchronously to adapt to your organization's needs.

As designed, Genre Boot Camp comprises an introduction to the Fiction List, a keynote speaker, a number of breakout sessions on specific genres, and an author visit. In 2013, ARRT presented eight breakout sessions, of which each of the 100 participants attended three. As mentioned earlier, the event could be adapted to suit a variety of audiences. In smaller communities, choosing to present a half-day program may be more feasible. By skipping the author visit and keynote address, organizers could fit three or four genre sessions into the schedule, which all participants would attend together. Or to keep the breadth of the program but avoid the time commitment of an entire workday, each session could be presented by an expert during a series of brown bag lunch meetings. To further reduce the stress of scheduling the event, technologically inclined organizers could record a series of webinars or videos to share with their colleagues asynchronously, perhaps introducing an online discussion forum to compensate for the lost participatory elements of an in-person event.

Regardless of format, each breakout session would be designed and presented by an expert in that genre, recruited by the event organizers. By acknowledging that even strong readers' advisors have strengths and weaknesses, ARRT organizers were able to capitalize on the strengths of professionals in their network. Even in academic or public libraries still developing their RA services, organizers may find avid readers who are experts in a particular genre. Expanding one's search to include booksellers could yield additional experts willing to share their knowledge of their favorite genres. And, of course, as information professionals, librarians without a particular passion for a genre could be tasked with researching the topic and developing an instructional session for their colleagues.

In terms of content for each breakout session, at the 2013 camp, each expert conducted a 40–45 minute presentation in which they gave an overview of the genre; distinguished between subgenres where necessary; highlighted resources for continued learning about the genre such as awards, best-of lists, or popular blogs; and noted any recent or anticipated trends. ARRT Steering

Committee members also created handouts for each genre in the Fiction List, which were distributed to speakers ahead of time and to all participants at the event. The goal of each session was to introduce attendees to the genre and give them the tools needed to stay abreast of important titles, authors, and trends.

Because Genre Boot Camp is a time- and staff-intensive endeavor, it could be a great opportunity to partner with public librarians in your area. The event itself could be initiated and organized by any librarian with an interest, regardless of RA knowledge. The key is identifying experts, whom you can find in public and academic libraries. The audience of the event could be diverse as well, including public and academic library professionals and paraprofessionals, MLS students, and bookstore employees. Scheduled breaks present opportunities for networking outside of the more formal presentations. In addition to the formal learning, attendees will get to know each other and their interests, learn from each other, and open doors for future collaborations.

ONGOING TRAINING OPPORTUNITIES

Librarians in any field seeking continuing education do not wait for invitations to participate in a class or attend a conference. They research opportunities, write proposals, and secure approvals and funding. The same approach should be taken for partnering with colleagues across the academic-public divide. Academic librarians looking to expand their knowledge of popular fiction and nonfiction should not hesitate to call their local public library and ask what types of training opportunities are available to their staff. Many libraries offer ongoing opportunities for their employees, from staff book discussions to genre studies to one-off trainings and more.

For libraries with ongoing opportunities, the investment of adding one or two additional participants to their programs is minimal. The attending librarian could take the new knowledge back to his or her library in a train the trainer model.[25] Or if the program is determined to be appropriate for the academic library's staff, the public librarian or librarians leading the training could be invited to repeat the training for the academic library staff. While this option requires more time from the public library staff involved, it would still be a minimal investment, as they have already expended the effort to develop the training materials.

If an academic librarian inquiring at the public library discovers there are no ongoing opportunities for staff there, this may be an opportunity to work with a key staff member at the public library to develop a joint training program that will benefit both libraries. The same obstacles that academic librarians face—time, budget constraints, and even lack of staff interest—can also be hurdles at public libraries. By sharing resources and staff expertise, both libraries can alleviate some of the burden that creating a new program entails while still providing quality training for their employees. It may even be stronger for the diversity of participants and the energy that bringing in new people and new ideas can infuse in a group.

PARTNERING IN PROGRAMMING AND OUTREACH

As mentioned in Chapter 4, book discussions can support the Slow Books movement on campus by creating space and time for reflection and promoting discourse. By collaborating with public libraries on campus book discussions, academic librarians can create additional opportunities for their students to develop lifelong learning habits and foster a love of reading.

An academic-public partnership for book discussions would be beneficial not only for the campus and community libraries but also the students. Having two moderators on a book discussion halves the workload for both librarians. With alternating moderators, a librarian is responsible for preparing background material, discussion questions, and further reading for only half of the year's offerings, while students and other participants get the benefit of a full year of discussions. Furthermore, having two moderators brings a diversity of taste and opinions that may help participants more fully explore ideas and themes contained in their reading. Multiple moderators also means more attention can be paid to each participant in the lulls before and after discussions, creating additional opportunities to make connections in the community.

One of the greatest benefits of book discussions for readers is the opportunity to build relationships with the librarian moderators. Library users who feel comfortable with staff are more likely to ask for reading suggestions, use the library regularly, and explore all that the library has to offer. For students in academic settings, their relationships with campus librarians will, at least to some extent, be limited by the student's eventual matriculation. Including a public librarian in discussions can help college students develop positive associations with the public library and continued usage as an adult. Whether they continue their lives after graduation in their college town or move to a new community, those positive associations would make public libraries more approachable and help negate a dip in library use common to this age group.

BEYOND BOOK DISCUSSIONS

The Slow Books movement need not be restricted to book discussions. Two of the goals of the Slow Books movement, as described by Meagan Lacy in Chapter 1, are to raise awareness about the value of books in the digital age and promote local writers and stories to build and sustain a literary arts community. While the mission and vision of many public libraries implicitly or explicitly call for the library to act as a community center or provide cultural programming, for many academic libraries, special events are a rarity. Here, too, are excellent opportunities for academic and public libraries to work together.

Where many libraries struggle in public programming is in engaging college-aged or post–college-aged adults. During their academic careers, most students use the academic library collection to meet research and, increasingly, leisure reading needs. Barbara Fister recognizes that academic libraries have not, traditionally, promoted the public library as an additional or postgraduation resource when she writes in Chapter 6:

> Institutions of higher education routinely make claims about preparation for lifelong learning, and libraries frequently frame information literacy as essential preparation for lifetime engagement with ideas and self-directed learning, yet we do little to encourage our students to include public library membership in their postgraduation plans, nor do we do much to prepare students to make use of information that isn't sought in response to a clearly articulated academic need.

While on campus, the academic library is and should be their primary resource. Once students graduate, however, the resources with which they have become comfortable are most often out of their reach.

Data suggest that students have trouble finding their way back to the public library after they have completed school but before they have children. The Pew Internet and American Life Project's 2012 study "Younger Americans' Reading and Library Habits" reports that while 74 percent of survey participants aged 25–29 said that the library was very important or somewhat important to them and their family,[26] only 54 percent of adults in the same age range had used the library in the past year.[27] Of the adults in that range who reported reading a book in the past year, only 8 percent had borrowed that title from the library.[28] Further data show that while most library users recognize the value of library programs for children and teens, adult programs have not elicited the same emotional response.[29] Partnerships between academic libraries with strong student-staff relationships and public libraries with programming experience can help bridge that gap and promote the library and, in turn, lifelong learning in their communities.

Successful events are about more than entertaining or informing audiences. At their best, they introduce library users to new ideas, like Slow Books, and new people, encouraging them to make connections among their neighbors and classmates, helping to build the literary community Lacy envisions. Moreover, staff-led events allow attendees to see library staff outside of an instruction session or without a reference desk between them. While many trends in library programming like makerspaces and nontraditional events are not directly related to the Slow Books movement, they are an important tool library staff can use to build relationships with individuals in the community. Those relationships can then encourage additional use of library services and materials and create advocates in the community who will vocally support the library. By encouraging the community to create space in their lives for regular library use, academic and public librarians can further support the Slow Books movement by developing readers in their communities.

In this arena, as with cross-training, there are a variety of approaches interested librarians could take to collaboration. On the simplest end of the scale, academic libraries can support public library programs by assisting with marketing efforts. Whether it is posting printed publicity in high-traffic areas in the library or helping identify key areas on campus to distribute information, the academic librarian has knowledge of student habits that the public librarian does not. Further assistance could be sharing the public library event on the library's social media outlets and library or campus events calendars. An even stronger method of support would be to help generate word of mouth by sharing exciting events with student workers and frontline staff in the library, and encouraging them to share it with library users they encounter. A genuine, personal invitation can be one of the best ways to entice a new event participant.

Partnerships can go beyond this level of professional courtesy, and they can go both ways. Any librarian planning an event for a college-aged audience would benefit from another brain during the planning process and another set of hands during the event. For many academic librarians, hosting events is outside of their normal scope, but they are well-versed in the needs and interests of the college students they serve. Public librarians, on the other hand, are likely to have more experience organizing events but are less adept at discerning the notoriously changeable tastes of the audience in question.

One might wonder how many professionals it takes to run an event, and if a partnership is necessary. While it is true that a wildly successful author visit, book discussion, or lecture could be managed by a single adept planner, there are trends in library events that call for more staff. From Human Libraries[30] to crafting, gardening, and seed swapping,[31] more libraries are experimenting with participatory events for adults of all ages. Monica Harris, in her article "The Power of Participatory," describes the Oak Park (Illinois) Public Library's initiative to develop more "patron-driven experiences" to balance traditional library programming and cites speed dating, adult spelling bees, and a pie-baking contest as examples.[32] She writes, "As our offerings got more creative we started to see new levels of investment from our customers as well as totally new faces at our library programs . . . the more we offered chances to share their own skills and passions, the more they felt connected to the library around them"[33]—and *books*, I would add.

Large-scale participatory events take more staff time. Consider a library hosting a spelling bee for adults.[34] Personnel needs include the pronouncer to read the words, give definitions, and so on; the judge to confirm spellings and be prepared to resolve disputes; the master of ceremonies to keep the event lively and on schedule; and the event runner to handle registration and sign in, greet attendees, monitor the schedule, support the other staff, and address problems as they arise. Though it is certainly possible to collapse duties and streamline the number of staff at events, distributing the responsibilities helps everyone manage stress and further allows participants to enjoy their evening. Especially if a major goal of an event is to help develop relationships with library staff, having adequate staff is essential for success. For many libraries, having four staff members on hand during an event may be impossible. Together, it becomes more manageable.

CONCLUSION

While it is easy to assume that academic and public librarians have different focuses and goals, there is much they can learn from each other. Academic librarians may balk at the many obstacles to beginning an RA practice, while public librarians have the advantage of experience and 30 years' worth of resources at their disposal. Public librarians struggle to reach the elusive college-aged and postcollege crowds, while academic librarians have, in some ways, a captive audience. Whether by developing readers' advisory practices or building relationships between library staff and community members, in bringing resources together, academic and public librarians can overcome obstacles like staff time and budgets to better guide emerging readers as they explore and develop their tastes and help potential readers find room in their lives for the library.

As seen in the absence of diverse partnerships in the literature, there are numerous opportunities for further exploration in this area. Libraries looking to build a successful partnership may consider some model of shared or floating collections; joint content creation on websites, blogs, and social media outlets; or further sharing of staff skills, perhaps through staff exchanges. Once a network has been established, potential partnerships between academic and public libraries are limited only by the imagination of the library staff and administration.

NOTES

1. Meagan Lacy and Emily States, "Going 'Slow:' Leading the Slow Books Movement at an Academic Library" (poster presented at the American Library Association, Chicago, IL, June 27–July 2, 2013. Available at http://hdl.handle.net/1805/3351.

2. Kathleen Halverson and Jean Plotas, "Creating and Capitalizing on the Town/Gown Relationship: An Academic Library and a Public Library Form a Community Partnership," *Journal of Academic Librarianship* 32, no. 6 (2006): 624–629.

3. Joan Giesecke, "The Value of Partnerships: Building New Partnerships for Success," *Journal of Library Administration* 52, no. 1 (2012): 37.

4. Schrage, Michael, *Shared Minds: The New Technologies of Collaboration* (New York: Random House, 1990), 40, quoted in Giesecke, "The Value of Partnerships," 36–52.

5. "SEFLIN Strategic Plan 2012–2017," SEFLIN, accessed December 21, 2013, https://dl.dropboxusercontent.com/u/51773410/eWeb percent20Docs/About percent 20SEFLIN percent20Page/Strategic_Plan_2012-2017_Update_10-18-2013.pdf.

6. "About the Library," Hawkeye Community College, accessed December 21, 2013, http://m.hawkeyecollege.edu/academics/library/about.aspx.

7. Halverson and Plotas, "Creating and Capitalizing on the Town/Gown Relationship," 627.

8. John N. Berry, "The San Jose State Model," *Library Journal* 129, no. 11 (2004): 34–37.

9. Stacy Brinkman and Frances Weinstein Yates, "Promoting Partnership: Campus and Community Collaboration through Cultural Events,"*College and Research Library News* 69, no. 3 (March 2008): 147–150, http://crln.acrl.org/content/69/3/147.full.pdf+html.

10. Ibid.

11. Ibid., 148.

12. Tom Wilding, "External Partnerships and Academic Libraries," *Library Management* 4/5, no. 23 (2002), 200.

13. Ibid.

14. Connie Van Fleet, "Popular Fiction Collections in Academic and Public Libraries," *Acquisitions Librarian* 29 (2003): 63–85.

15. Pauline Dewan, "Reading Matters in the Academic Library: Taking the Lead from Public Librarians," *Reference and User Services Quarterly* 52, no. 4 (2013): 309–319.

16. Mikics, David, *Slow Reading in a Hurried Age* (Cambridge, MA: Belknap Press of Harvard University Press, 2013), 39.

17. S. R. Ranganathan, *The Five Laws of Library Science* (Madras: Madras Library Association, 1931), http://hdl.handle.net/2027/uc1.$b99721.

18. Mikics, *Slow Reading in a Hurried Age*, 39.

19. Ibid., 55.

20. Melanie A. Kimball, "A Brief History of Readers' Advisory," in *Genreflecting*, ed. Wayne A. Wiegand (Westport, CT: Libraries Unlimited, 2006), 18.

21. "Adult Reading Round Table Mission Statement & Bylaws," Adult Reading Round Table, accessed April 8, 2014, http://www.arrtreads.org/images/Mission_Statement_and_Bylaws_2012.pdf.

22. *The ARRT Popular Fiction List: A Self-Evaluative Bibliography for Readers Advisors*, 4th ed. ([Geneva, IL]: Adult Reading Round Table, 2012). The ARRT Popular Fiction List is available to subscribers of NoveList Plus in the Readers' Advisory Toolbox, and is also available for purchase at http://arrtreads.org/popularfictionlists.html.

23. Ibid., 4.

24. Ibid.

25. For an overview of one such program that could be adapted and scaled to benefit libraries or library groups of varying sizes, see Sherrey Quinn, "Reading Rewards: The Evolution of a Train the Trainer Course for Public Library Reader Advisers," *APLIS* 21, no. 2 (2008): 44–55.

26. Kathryn Zickuhr et al., *Younger Americans' Reading and Library Habits* (Washington D.C.: Pew Internet and American Life Project, 2012), 12, accessed January 28, 2014, http://libraries.pewinternet.org/files/legacy-pdf/PIP_YoungerLibraryPatrons.pdf.

27. Ibid., 11.

28. Ibid., 36.

29. Kathryn Zickuhr, Lee Rainie, and Kristin Purcell, *Library Services in the Digital Age* (Washington D.C.: Pew Internet and American Life Project, 2013) discuss reported reasons for increase or decrease in library usage over the past year. Of the 26 percent of users who reported an increase in their library use, only 4 percent of users reported library events and activities as a reason they've increased their library use, while 26 percent said they enjoy taking their children or grandchildren—the most popular response for that question. In that same study, of the 53 percent of respondents who visited a library or bookmobile in the past 12 months, 41 percent said they visited "to attend or bring a younger person to a class, program, or event designed for children or teens," while only 21 percent said they visited "to attend a class, program, or lecture for adults." Of the 22 percent of respondents who noted a decrease in their library use, 16 percent said "the library is not as useful because my children have grown, I'm retired, I'm no longer a student." Based on these data, one can conclude that many library users value the event offerings for children and teens more than they value those for adults.

30. Erin Wentz, "The Human Library: Sharing the Community with Itself," *Public Libraries* 51 no. 3 (2012): 38–40.

31. Lian Sze, "Tales from the Front: Programming that Packs the Place," *Public Libraries* 51 no. 4 (2012): 14–16.

32. Monica Harris, "The Power of Participatory," *ILA Reporter* 21, no. 2 (2013): 24–25, http://www.ila.org/Reporter/April_2013/Reporter_0413.pdf.

33. Ibid., 24.

34. Three such spelling bees were hosted at Oak Park Public Library as part of our genre X programming. See genre-x.com for more information.

11

REDEFINING "IMPOSSIBLE": A PUBLIC LIBRARY'S JOURNEY THROUGH THE CLASSICS

Karen Hansen and Lesley Williams

"Classic." A book which people praise and don't read.

—*Mark Twain,* Pudd'nhead Wilson's New Calendar in Following the Equator

The best of intentions don't always get the job done, and such is the case when it comes to reading the classics. This is why so many educated, otherwise well-rounded people have dusty, once-opened copies of amazing, challenging books on their shelves: *Ulysses*, *War and Peace*, *Crime and Punishment*, *In Search of Lost Time*, *Middlemarch*, *Moby-Dick*, and many more. We know reading classic literature is good for us in a rich and satisfying way because, after all, these books have endured the test of time. Why, then, do so many people stop at good intentions?

A handful of librarians at the Evanston Public Library discovered they shared this dilemma: wanting to read great literature doesn't always translate into actually reading it. For us, James Joyce's *Ulysses* was the top book on our reading wish lists, and we realized that we certainly weren't alone: many otherwise well-educated people have made unsuccessful attempts to scale literary "Everests" such as *Ulysses*. The problem, we decided, was that we had attempted these feats *alone*. Good intentions were not enough to make it to the last "yes" in *Ulysses*. To meet the challenge, we determined we needed a support group, and thus, our Mission Impossible book group was born. Our motto thus became: "One Book. One Year. One Mission: Finish." Neither a Great Books Club, nor a "One Book, One Community" program, Mission Impossible had a simple goal: to provide opportunity and support for adult readers in our community to engage with challenging and life-changing works of literature. We also decided that fellow readers may want to make the journey through *Ulysses* slowly and thoughtfully, in such a way that reading the novel wouldn't monopolize our reading time. Therefore, in our planning for Mission Impossible: *Ulysses*, we spread meetings over the course of an entire year. After months of promoting our newly minted Mission Impossible book group, we expected a turnout of no more than 30 at our opening lecture at the Irish pub across from our main library. To our utter surprise, we arrived to find the room crowded, with a line out the door and more people still arriving. That night, more than 110 people joined our program. This is how we began our surprising journey into the Slow Books movement at the Evanston Public Library on Bloomsday 2010. Since then, hundreds of people have participated in Mission Impossible, and we've successfully tackled four other classics: *War and Peace*, *The Complete Stories: Flannery O'Connor*, and volumes I and II of Proust's *In Search of Lost Time*. We're confident that what happened in our community is not an anomaly, and that libraries—small and large, public and academic—can find readers in their community who wish to engage in reading challenging literature together.

OUR JOURNEY THROUGH FOUR CLASSICS

Our opening lecture for *Ulysses* confirmed that we weren't alone in our desire to read challenging books, and, more importantly, it revealed an untapped need in our community. In response to the overwhelming interest in the program, we quickly rescaled it by recruiting several more group leaders and finding additional meeting spaces—including the Irish pub across the street. Our five group leaders consisted of librarians, paraprofessionals, and a community volunteer, and, as it turned out, only one of them had actually read *Ulysses* cover to cover. We were simply grateful that anyone would agree to read the novel and lead a group at all, so prior experience was not required; in fact, we saw that as in keeping with our "populist" approach. Most leaders were assigned groups of about 15, although our pub groups swelled to as many as 30 participants. To streamline meeting times and provide reluctant leaders with extra support, all groups had the same reading assignments, and all meetings occurred during the same week during each discussion cycle. One point person would also share a bank of discussion questions with leaders. To further ease the burden of these meetings on our library staff, we spaced meetings to occur once every two months. For some participants, having extra time in between meetings helped them feel free to read other books and make assignments less of a chore. For others, however, too much time in between meetings made it harder for them to connect with the reading.

We were delighted and intrigued with how participants engaged with the text socially. When we started with *Ulysses*, hardly anyone knew each other outside the library, and most were entirely new to our library-sponsored book groups. After the first session or two, however, people definitely began to bond around the shared experience of journeying through the challenging text. Soon, seeing other group members at meetings became a strong motivator for many participants to finish assignments—positive peer pressure. Even though the reading was difficult and confusing—the reason many people reading alone would quit—members slogged right on through. As many of us learned, clarity came with discussion, so we became comfortable with the idea that we didn't have to understand everything alone.

The sense of place also affected the dynamic of our discussions. While most discussion sections met at library locations, two of them met in the party room at the Irish pub nearby. The library groups followed a much more traditional framework of leader-led discussions, but the ones that met at the pub took on a more casual, peer-led dynamic. Everyone had a list of discussion starters, and each table was responsible for guiding the conversation. The leader would rove from table to table. The pub atmosphere felt like having a meal and a beer with friends, where the topic of conversation happened to be *Ulysses* each time. Meetings were relaxed and fun for all, and talking about the book felt natural and easy. For one meeting, our evening pub group had to be moved to the library, and the change in atmosphere was distinct: everyone looked to the leader for direction and insight, and things felt a bit more strained compared to discussions at the pub. Overall, having several types of locations was a bonus because it meant there was a place to meet just about every need.

Along with our regular discussion sessions, we added related programs and incentives to enrich the Mission Impossible experience. We brought back our Northwestern professor, who had delivered our kickoff lecture, to help with a particularly challenging portion of the novel, and we also invited a local artist to display his "36 Views of *Ulysses*" exhibit. Midway through the program, we gave away buttons with a variety of humorous sayings, (e.g., "I Heart Garryowens") related to *Ulysses* to encourage the remaining members. To cap off our first Mission Impossible, we held a Bloomsday celebration of readings, Irish music, giveaways (including real lemon soap from Ireland), and a lively game of "Joyce Jeopardy." Those who completed the program were awarded a certificate of achievement, which many folks still proudly display in their homes. Participants could also purchase souvenir mugs we designed for the occasion. All of these activities and incentives helped make Mission Impossible meaningful, memorable, and, most importantly, fun. After all, you're probably missing something if you can't read most classics and laugh along the way.

By the time our journey through *Ulysses* concluded, roughly half (or about 60) of our participants finished, a percentage we consider very successful. The other half left the program gradually throughout the year, usually because they grew too busy to keep up with the reading, found it too challenging, or simply couldn't connect with the novel. We dubbed those who remained "The Few, The Proud, The Persistent." One of the most significant soft markers of our program's success was the question we received constantly: "What are we reading next?" With so many votes of confidence, we chose to continue Mission Impossible indefinitely.

After *Ulysses*, we opted to tackle *War and Peace*. Apparently, our *Ulysses* members were so enthusiastic about the program, they told their friends. Our next kickoff lecture was packed to the brim with 160 in attendance. We offered 10 discussion sections in total, and even that was not enough to keep up with demand. Once we launched *War and Peace*, we had community groups, including one from our city's senior center, asking us to help support additional groups. Along with our two pub groups, we expanded our nonlibrary meeting locations to include a cupcake shop and the local Barnes & Noble. *War and Peace* followed the same centralized structure as *Ulysses*, supporting consistency with meeting times, locations, and reading assignments. Although *War and Peace* is longer than *Ulysses*, it's a quicker, more plot-driven read, so we condensed the last reading assignments and finished in 10 months. Due to popular demand, we again offered a certificate and a souvenir—this time, shot glasses. By the end of our journey through *War and Peace*, 90 readers, or again roughly half, had finished.

For our third mission, because participants expressed a greater desire to meet monthly, we experimented with an even more condensed version. For a more user-driven experience, we selected a handful of potential works and enabled patrons to vote for our next selection.

Our participants voted to read *The Complete Stories: Flannery O'Connor*. In this departure from the long novel format, we experimented with running a shorter program in three consecutive months, instead of our yearlong format. Attendance was slightly lower than for our previous programs—at 120 participants—but we kept all other aspects the same: opening lecture, multiple groups reading the same assignments, and a souvenir item for those who finished. As in years past, roughly half completed the book. The short stories were easy to build upon for each meeting and nurtured many thematic discussions. Group members also enjoyed the more condensed reading schedule.

Three years after the inception of Mission Impossible, we opted to take on the humbling challenge of Marcel Proust's *In Search of Lost Time*, a massive, seven-volume tome. Rather than read all seven volumes at once, however, we thought it prudent to start with the first two and take a year to read them. Perhaps because of the utterly intimidating reputation of *In Search of Lost Time*, fewer people—85—signed up to read it. We kept our every-other-month format and added an extra supplemental lecture for good measure. The result was much the same as our other programs: half finished. Many participants expressed that they were pleasantly surprised with Proust. They enjoyed it much more than they had anticipated they would and even wished to continue reading the next volume of the novel! To accommodate this small—but enthusiastic—crowd, we'll be sponsoring an offshoot "Super Proust" group in addition to continuing on with our next Mission Impossible selection: *Middlemarch.*

We will note that throughout our four Mission Impossible programs, our groups have mainly attracted a more mature demographic of middle-aged people and retirees, and mostly women. Younger professionals do come to some of the groups, but there is more to be done to attract those in their twenties and thirties. Men certainly come to our groups, but they make up only about a quarter of our participants. A stronger partnership with Northwestern University may help diversify our groups in terms of age and gender. Other ideas include selecting a more contemporary classic or changing up our meeting times and locations.

HOW TO START A MISSION IMPOSSIBLE PROGRAM

Starting a Mission Impossible program at your library—no matter its size or type—can be a reality if you're first willing to reconsider your expectations of what your patrons expect out of the library and what your patrons aspire to read. So often, librarians assume many things about their patrons—that they neither have the time nor the desire to read long and challenging pieces of literature, and certainly not with a library book club! If you can shed those preconceived notions, you're ready to give Mission Impossible a try. After completing four rounds of Mission Impossible, we've developed a few key principles for setting the stage for a successful program.

First and foremost, chose books people *want* to read! There are plenty of classics fitting Mark Twain's famous epigram defining the "classic." Although we've heard a few pleas for *Autocrat of the Breakfast Table* or *The Complete Works of Aeschylus*, it was not our goal to shove great literature down any throats. Our initial choice, *Ulysses*, may be famous for its obscurity and difficulty, yet it is also greatly beloved, with a rabid international fan base. Clearly, there is a reason for this adoration. With that in mind, it's best to choose based on the following criteria: (1) the work is revered, (2) people want to read it, and (3) it's intimidating to read on one's own because of its length or challenging content.

Don't rush through the reading—slow down! This should be pretty self-explanatory, but it's not the norm for most book groups. Spread reading assignments over a few months or even a year, depending on the commitment and availability of your group members and library staff. Reading a novel like *Ulysses* may seem like the literary equivalent of climbing Mount Everest. That's why we break each novel we read into manageable sections, taking on the mountain one molehill at a time. Reading assignments are typically 150 to 300 pages—the novel roughly divided by the number of scheduled meetings. When devising assignments, we also recommend taking into account a book's natural breaks if chapters don't do the job for you.

In keeping with a slower pace, consider spacing meetings a bit further apart—meet once every six weeks or once every other month. This gives your participants the freedom to read other books while reading a Mission Impossible selection. Reading a challenging book should not be an all-or-nothing endeavor. Spacing sessions can also give staff more room to pursue other projects and lead other discussion groups without feeling overwhelmed. In deciding how frequently to meet, however, you may also want to factor in the density of your reading material. For us, the every-other-month model worked especially well for the intense and rigorous *Ulysses*, but we found it didn't always fit well for the more plot-driven *War and Peace*.

If something like *Ulysses* just seems too daunting, why not warm up with a shorter work? Tackling a shorter novel over a few months may be an appealing alternative. Staff and patrons may also appreciate a confidence-building exercise before heading up the mountain. Shorter works to consider are *Moby-Dick*, *Middlemarch*, *Anna Karenina*, or *The Brothers Karamazov*, just to name a few. Other options for a more abbreviated series include doing a collection of short stories or a few novels by the same author: Ernest Hemingway, William Faulkner, and so on. A book's length isn't everything, though. *Ulysses*, for example, weighs in at about 800 pages but takes a long time to complete because of its density. A more plot-driven novel of the same length may be accomplished in a much shorter amount of time.

Just as you are what you eat, you are where you meet. Your meeting location may dictate the overall tone of your book group, so choose accordingly. A meeting room with a conference table may lend itself well to a traditional, leader-led format, and groups who need a lot of direction with a text may crave this type of leadership. Plus, a formal environment can help keep distractions and digressions to a minimum. On the other hand, consider finding meeting locations outside of the library to nurture a more peer-led, relaxed dynamic. Bookstores, cafés, and pubs can be great locations, especially if they can offer a small room or space that's a bit quieter. Talking about a book over a drink and a warm meal simply feels more natural to many people. In addition to nurturing a more relaxed discussion environment, using businesses as meeting places is a great way to build community partnerships. These businesses enjoy the visibility and the patronage from participants, and participants benefit from the change of pace.

Take the time to thoroughly promote your Mission Impossible group. Well in advance of your first meeting, start marketing the program—both online and in print, inside and outside of the library. We used a combination of all of these tools to get the word out about Mission Impossible, and the result was that we drew in many library users and nonusers alike. If you start marketing the program six to eight weeks ahead of time, you can also give potential participants more time to do some powerful word-of-mouth marketing for you. In fact, in two short surveys we gave to our outgoing *Ulysses* and Proust participants, roughly 20–30 percent of respondents reported that they heard about the program through a friend or family member.

Take advantage of local expertise. We have been fortunate to have the enthusiastic support of several wonderful faculty members at Northwestern and Loyola Universities. Literary academics are generally delighted to speak about their favorite authors, and we have been able to secure excellent speakers each year for free. The only difficulty was in convincing potential speakers that we actually had a huge group of community residents eager to hear them discuss the social setting of Proust, Flannery O'Connor's works, or the role of the Napoleonic Wars in Tolstoy. Each and every one of these speakers was completely surprised and refreshed to impart their expertise on such an eager audience.

Enhance your group's journey through a challenging book with a blog, Facebook page, Twitter, or other online communication tool. Harnessing one of these tools can help keep your participants engaged in the text between meetings. Our groups gravitated toward our blogs, which we maintained for each Mission Impossible program.[1] We posted interesting facts, information about the author, historical details, and other miscellanea, as well as more practical communications and announcements. Many participants subscribed to the blog for each program. We also tried other online outlets and put up a Facebook fan page, with the hope participants would discuss the readings online. The page didn't catch on very well with our members, but it may take off better for other groups who have more interest in Facebook or who have a younger member base. Twitter may also be a great choice for patrons who want to discuss the book in chunks of 140 or fewer characters. One does not need to look far on the Internet for examples of how to use Twitter for book clubs. One of the best examples is the *Atlantic* magazine's @1book140 (formerly @1b1t, or One Book, One Twitter).

Use your library reference skills. Mission Impossible is a great way to promote the collection, enabling readers to delve into questions of social class, evolution of artistic taste and genres, religion, even fashion. We've offered companion sources on Russia's serfs; the Napoleonic wars; the Irish Independence movement; anti-Semitism in Ireland, Russia, and France; racism in the South; the role of the "demi-mondaine" in France; and the Dreyfus affair. We also steer readers toward a variety of online resources such as Goodreads, (which has thriving online discussions of all the novels we've covered), Khan Academy (great for videos on the relevant historical periods), and specialized sources like Ulysses Seen, or Proust Ink.

Give some time and consideration to the physical book itself. Should your library purchase enough copies of your selection for every member? Should you recommend a specific edition? These two questions may carry more weight than you'd think. Because of the scale of our programs, we purchased no more than 30 copies for any given program—in most cases, only enough copies for 20 percent of our participants. However, if your group has only

30 participants, maybe buying a copy for every person is within your budget, or within the budget of a donor or a friends group. We also chose not to buy more copies because we wanted participants to feel a greater sense of ownership and commitment to their reading, as well as have the freedom to mark their own copies. Few people complained about this decision. The question of which edition to use can also be a difficult one. Allowing your participants to choose any edition can be fine if your participants have their own copies already, editions don't vary greatly in terms of pagination, or if the book was originally published in English. We have tried both approaches, but we've experienced the greatest amount of success when we recommend just one edition. It's more streamlined, far easier when planning a reading schedule, and makes it much simpler during discussions when referring to a particular passage.

Finally, the single most important principle to a successful Mission Impossible program is social support. Call it positive peer pressure or call it the buddy system, but either way, we cannot emphasize how big a role it plays in motivating patrons to join Mission Impossible and to stick with it to the end. Reading with social support provides accountability and a reason to meet a goal. This is the whole reason we started Mission Impossible: because we had failed to finish a challenging book alone. The social element also enables participants to understand difficult material through discussion itself, a phenomenon nearly any book group leader has witnessed and experienced. With the dependability of community support, participants often grow comfortable with the discomfort the text can bring. We would often remind people that it's okay to feel confused about certain passages—that we might all be confused—and that discussion can help clarify our understanding of the text. If there's one important thing to convey to market the group to a potential participant or even to encourage a current participant, it's this community of support. Anything feels less daunting when you're all in the same boat.

ADAPTING MISSION IMPOSSIBLE TO AN ACADEMIC SETTING

Why should an academic library consider adapting a Mission Impossible program? At its core, Mission Impossible is about nurturing lifelong learning, a goal entirely compatible with the objectives of higher education. For many students, however, becoming lifelong learners won't be enough to convince them to pile more on their plates, which are already full of lectures, reading assignments, research papers, and social engagements. For a more meaningful academic experience, though, students *must* take in more than just the meat and potatoes of university life. Whereas we often compare Mission Impossible to an athletic feat in the public library, like climbing a mountain or running a marathon, for students, it might be best to compare it more to eating. To get the most out of life, you don't just eat for sustenance, you eat to savor. For students, Mission Impossible can be a warm, richly spiced, literary banquet, the unexpectedly delicious meal discovered at a restaurant with a forbidding exterior.

To entice students to try a different literary fare, avoid presenting Mission Impossible as a class. There are two things Mission Impossible is not: it is not a for-credit class, and it is not a Great Books program. Classes have expert instructors. Great Books programs have trained leaders who are expected to follow a prescribed format. Mission Impossible is participatory: the leaders are learning right alongside the other readers. We also caution against the classroom format because we avoid presenting challenging literature negatively and prescriptively, as an unpleasant but necessary "medicine" one must take in order to improve one's mind.

One way to keep discussions flexible, participatory, and fun is to hold meetings off campus or at least at a low-key, relaxed location. As previously mentioned, cafés, restaurants, pubs, and bookstores are all great choices. Leaving campus can help students get out of the classroom mode and into another mindset. Though it sounds cliché, enjoying food and drink together can really set the tone for a warmer, more low-key discussion than would be experienced in a classroom.

Reach out across disciplines when recruiting potential participants and move beyond the easy targets: English majors. We are big proponents of a "no literary background necessary" approach, so try to shed the expectation that only people studying literature will be interested in reading a challenging novel. Again, our participants represent people from a spectrum of occupations. Perhaps there's a chemistry major out there who wants a change of pace without the commitment of a class? If your reading selection lends itself to enrichment with art or music, find ways to engage students from those disciplines as well. Encourage students to create artwork inspired by the book or engage with a musical composition mentioned in the book.

Tap into the expertise of professors and other knowledgeable people in the community. Obviously, an academic setting is rich with people and resources to draw from to enhance the reading experience. These folks can help supplement a Mission Impossible program with their expertise through lectures and so on. They may even do a little word-of-mouth marketing for you! While these folks may be a wonderful resource for enriching your program, you may want to steer away from recruiting experts as group leaders. If your readers are reluctant, participants may feel most at ease with someone reading the book for the first time, too.

A major challenge to adapting Mission Impossible to an academic setting is time—both in terms of the amount students have to devote to extra activities and in terms of scheduling the program. Since students are generally strapped for extra time, choosing a shorter, more plot-driven work may work best. Scheduling when the program will begin and end also deserves special consideration. Midterms and final exams are significant obstacles. You may even experiment with offering Mission Impossible to students on campus during the summer. This is where a brief survey might come in handy to find out what is the best time of year for a program.

Consider partnering with your local public library. As we have demonstrated in Evanston, connecting a university with Mission Impossible can be a natural way to build a relationship with your local public library, and even more than that, cultivate positive town/gown relations. Doing Mission Impossible together can spice up programming, promote cross-promotion and marketing, and reflect good public relations for all involved. This is also a good opportunity to encourage students to get involved with their own community—not just the academic community, but the community at large.

Don't forget to nurture the social ties of Mission Impossible, since they can be the glue that keeps your group reading on to the end. After all, many students thrive on social connection, so use any tools necessary to keep it fresh—social media, enriching events and lectures, and so on. Without emphasizing this support, Mission Impossible may become just another class.

FINAL THOUGHTS

When we first conceived of the idea of running a library book group devoted to reading *Ulysses*, many people (fellow librarians included) laughed and proclaimed that no one would show up. Years later, the program is still going strong, and with hundreds who have finished great classics, people no longer laugh when we tell them of the success of Mission Impossible.

It's time to challenge our perceptions of what people want to read and what they want out of the library itself. Although we understand that what we've done can't be replicated everywhere, we believe we've succeeded in defying traditional ideas of what people are capable of reading. What we've accomplished demonstrates that people may be hungry for a more substantial literary fare and that many people in our communities have a desire to tackle very difficult literature without the cost and commitment of taking a class. The Mission Impossible program can be a venue for them to do so. At our library, we believe the program has placed our library in a very advantageous position. We've tapped into a previously undiscovered need in our community—and by tapping into this need we're continuing to build the library's reputation as *the* place to find enrichment—intellectually, socially, and culturally. As a final thought, consider Supreme Court Justice Stephen Breyer's brilliant statement on the enduring value of great literature:

> I've always thought that it was not particularly useful to study law as an undergrad. We are only allowed to live one life: it's the human condition, there's no escaping it. In my view, only by studying the humanities can we hope to escape this fundamental limitation and understand how other people live. Because literature, history, or philosophy all provide extraordinary windows on the world.[2]

NOTES

1. See "Mission Impossible: Ulysses," http://missionimpossibleulysses.wordpress.com/; "Mission Impossible: War and Peace," http://missionimpossiblewarandpeace.wordpress.com/; "Mission Impossible: Flannery O'Connor," http://missionimpossibleoconnor.wordpress.com/, "Mission Impossible: Proust," http://missionimpossibleproust.wordpress.com/.

2. Stephen Breyer, "On Reading Proust," *New York Review of Books*, November 7, 2013, accessed January 13, 2014, http://www.nybooks.com/articles/archives/2013/nov/07/reading-proust/.

CONCLUSION

It's Friday morning, and I am alone in my office, staring at my computer, trying to find the words that will neatly tie up this book. Meanwhile, my iPhone is blowing up with text messages—I'm going to see *American Hustle* tomorrow night, instead of tonight, in case you are interested—and my Outlook keeps dinging and cluttering my computer screen with pop-ups.

I am struggling, in other words, to concentrate.

I mention these details so as to emphasize just how insidious these digital distractions have become. I am struggling to reflect on a book that insists on the value and importance of creative reflection. I am struggling to *do my job.* As David Levy observes in his article "No Time to Think: Reflections on Information Technology and Contemplative Scholarship," the accelerated pace of life induced by new information and communication technologies has bled into university culture, endangering the reflective practices and deep thinking that are foundational to its existence.[1] As someone who has researched, written, and edited this book while also trying to be a good librarian, teacher, and colleague, I can appreciate this problem. Even without the din of dinging digital devices, it is hard to find the quiet to think.

As a response, Levy calls on universities "to bring contemplative practices explicitly into university curricula to help students, faculty, and staff strengthen their attentional faculties in the face of the erosion effected by multitasking and acceleration."[2] In other words, we, the educators, must model contemplative practices if we hope for our students to adopt and develop these practices for themselves. Marilee Sprenger concretely suggests that we model attentive listening and teach meditative techniques that promote mindfulness.[3]

The Slow Books movement meets these demands. Again, reading books, especially challenging works of literature, forces one to slow down and . . . think. It *is* a meditative technique. Furthermore, as the librarians and educators who have contributed chapters to this volume have shown, there are many ways that libraries can nurture youth's contemplative practices and provide them with "spaces for sustained reflection and authentic connection."[4] Book club discussions, One Book One Community programming, and for-credit reading courses all give students sanctioned time and space for reflection and opportunities to practice discussion and attentive listening. These strategies literally change the rules of engagement, from online to in person, so that students can focus on themselves and their own thinking, self-reflect, and strike a balance between connecting with technology and connecting with real people.

Public libraries ensure that this practice continues throughout their lifetime. Already the leaders in readers' advisory, public libraries ensure that no one suffers from reader's block. But, they could also add Slow Books to their menu of readers' advisory services. By encouraging patrons to try challenging works of literature and by supporting them in this endeavor, as Karen Hansen and Lesley Johnson exemplify at the Evanston Public Library, they not only enhance their existing reader's services but also continue to promote and model contemplative practice, which is *as* essential to work, democracy, and everyday living as it is to university culture.

Finally, through collaborative partnerships, we can expand the Slow Books movement and deepen its impact—and perhaps change our culture's attitudes toward reading and speed. To echo Guy Montag in Ray Bradbury's *Fahrenheit 451*, "An hour a day, two hours, with these books, and maybe . . ."[5] Maybe we'd be happier.

At least, we can pose the question, "Why *must* we be in a rush?" Certainly, speed has its advantages. But when it comes to some things—things that affect our intellectual, physical, and emotional health—speed might not be relevant, or even appropriate. Slow Books, like other slow movements, remind us that we have a choice, and have always had a choice, to pause and to reflect and to dictate the pace of our own lives. Our quality of life, our happiness, might depend on it.

By now, I hope that your mind is wandering from this page and into your own imagination. I hope that you will take the ideas gathered here and develop them further—improve them, transform them, and share them—to bring the Slow Books movement to your library and beyond.

NOTES

1. David M. Levy, "No Time to Think: Reflections on Information Technology and Contemplative Scholarship," *Ethics and Information Technology* 9, no. 4 (2007): 237–249.
2. Ibid., 248.
3. Marilee Sprenger, "Focusing the Digital Brain," *Educational Leadership* 67, no. 1 (2009): 34–39.
4. Katie Davis, "A Life in Bits and Bytes: A Portrait of a College Student and Her Life with Digital Media," *Teachers College Record* 113, no. 9 (2011): 1960–1982.
5. Ray Bradbury, *Fahrenheit 451* (New York: Simon & Schuster, 2012), 70.

Further Reading

READER'S ADVISORY AND READING

Alpert, Abby. "Incorporating Nonfiction into Readers' Advisory Services." *Reference & User Services Quarterly* 46, no. 1 (2006): 25–32.

Berrett, Dan. "Students May Be Reading Plenty, But Much of It Is Not for Class." *Chronicle of Higher Education* 59, no. 35 (2013): A6.

Block, Cathy Collins, and John N Mangieri. "Recreational Reading: 20 Years Later." *Reading Teacher* 55, no. 6 (2002): 572–80.

Cullinan, Bernice E. "Independent Reading and School Achievement." *School Library Media Research* 3 (2000): 1–24. http://www.ala.org/aasl/aaslpubsandjournals/slmrb/slmrcontents/volume32000/independent#effects.

De Rosa, Cathy, Joanne Cantrell, Janet Hawk, and Alane Wilson. "College Students' Perceptions of Libraries and Information Resources." 2006. http://www.mendeley.com/catalog/college-students-perceptions-libraries-information-resources/.

Dewan, Pauline. "Reading Matters in the Academic Library: Taking the Lead from Public Librarians." *Reference & User Services Quarterly* 52, no. 4 (2013): 309–19.

Dewan, Pauline. "Why Your Academic Library Needs a Popular Reading Collection Now More Than Ever." *College & Undergraduate Libraries* 17, no. 1 (2010): 44–64. doi:10.1080/10691310903584775.

Elliott, Julie. "Academic Libraries and Extracurricular Reading Promotion." *Reference & User Services Quarterly* 46, no. 3 (2007): 34–43. http://rusa.metapress.com/index/KV13W82R07067111.pdf.

Elliott, Julie. "Barriers to Extracurricular Reading Promotion in Academic Libraries." *Reference & User Services Quarterly* 48, no. 4 (2009): 340–47. http://rusa.metapress.com/index/M170M6U588383R68.pdf.

Gilbert, Julie, and Barbara Fister. "Reading, Risk, and Reality: College Students and Reading for Pleasure." *College & Research Libraries* 72 (2011): 474–95.

Krashen, Stephen D. *Power of Reading: Insights from the Research*. Westport, CT: Libraries Unlimited, 2004.

MacAdam, Barbara. "Sustaining the Culture of the Book: The Role of Enrichment Reading and Critical Thinking in the Undergraduate Curriculum." *Library Trends* 44, no. 2 (1995): 237–64.

Manguel. Alberto. *A History of Reading*. Toronto, ON: Vintage Canada, 1998.

National Endowment for the Arts. "To Read or Not to Read: A Question of National Consequence." 2007. http://arts.endow.gov/research/ToRead.pdf.

Rathe, Bette, and Lisa Blankenship. "Recreational Reading Collections in Academic Libraries." *Collection Management* 30, no. 2 (2005): 73–85. doi:10.1300/J105v30n02.

Ross, Catherine Sheldrick. "Finding without Seeking: What Readers Say about the Role of Pleasure Reading as a Source of Information." *Australasian Public Libraries and Information Services* 13, no. 2 (2000): 72–80.

Ross, Catherine Sheldrick. "Making Choices: What Readers Say about Choosing Books to Read for Pleasure." *Acquisitions Librarian* 13, no. 25 (2001): 5–21.

Ross, Catherine Sheldrick. "Reader on Top: Public Libraries, Pleasure Reading, and Models of Reading." *Library Trends* 57, no. 4 (2009): 632–56.

Ross, Catherine Sheldrick. "Reading Nonfiction for Pleasure." In *Nonfiction Readers' Advisory*, edited by Robert Burgin, 105–20. Westport, CT: Libraries Unlimited, 2004.

Ross, Catherine Sheldrick, and Mary K Chelton. "Reader's Advisory : Matching Mood and Material." *Library Journal*, February 1, 2001: 52–55.

Ross, Catherine Sheldrick, Lynne (E. F.) McKechnie, and Paulette Rothbauer. *Reading Matters: What the Research Reveals about Reading, Libraries, and Community*. Westport, CT: Libraries Unlimited, 2006.

Saricks, Joyce, G. *Readers' Advisory Service in the Public Library*. 3rd ed. Chicago: American Library Association, 2005.

Schank, Roger C., and Tamara R. Berman. "The Pervasive Role of Stories in Knowledge and Action." In *Narrative Impact: Social and Cognitive Foundations*, edited by Melanie C. Green, Jeffrey J. Strange, and Timothy C. Brock, 287–313. Mahwah, NJ: L. Erlbaum Associates, 2002.

Shearer, Kenneth D. "The Appeal of Nonfiction: A Tale of Many Tastes." In *Nonfiction Readers' Advisory*, edited by Robert Burgin, 67–83. Westport, CT: Libraries Unlimited, 2004.

Smith, Rochelle, and Nancy J. Young. "Giving Pleasure Its Due: Collection Promotion and Readers' Advisory in Academic Libraries."*Journal of Academic Librarianship* 34, no. 6 (2008): 520–26. doi:10.1016/j.acalib.2008.09.003.

Staley, Lissa. "Passive Readers' Advisory: Bookmarks, Booklists, and Displays." In *The Readers' Advisory Handbook*, edited by Jessica E. Moyer and Kaite Mediatore Stover, 73–80. Chicago: American Library Association, 2010.

Trott, Barry. "Reference, Readers' Advisory, and Relevance." *Reference Librarian* 53, no. 1 (2012): 60–66. doi:10.1080/02763877.2011.596367.

Van Riel, Rachel, Olive Fowler, and Anne Downes. *The Reader-Friendly Library Service*. Newcastle upon Tyne, UK: Society of Chief Librarians, 2008.

Van Riel, Rachel. "Whichbook." http://www.openingthebook.com/whichbook/.

Woodward, Jeannette. *Creating the Customer-Driven Academic Library*. Chicago: American Library Association, 2009.

Woodward, Jeannette. *Creating the Customer-Driven Library: Building on the Bookstore Model*. Chicago: American Library, 2005.

Wyatt, Neal. *The Readers' Advisory Guide to Nonfiction*. Chicago: American Library Association, 2007.

Zauha, Janelle M. 1993. "Recreational Reading in Academic Browsing Rooms." *Collection Building* 12, no. 3–4 (1993): 57–62.

RA PRINT TOOLS

Genrefecting Series

Bosman, Ellen, John P. Bradford, and Robert B. Ridinger. *Gay, Lesbian, Bisexual, and Transgendered Literature: A Genre Guide.* Westport, CT: Libraries Unlimited, 2008.

Cords, Sarah Statz. *The Real Story: A Guide to Nonfiction Reading Interests.* Westport, CT: Libraries Unlimited, 2006.

Dawson, Alma. *African American Literature: A Guide to Reading Interests.* Westport, CT: Libraries Unlimited, 2004.

Fonseca, Anthony J., and June Michele Pulliam. *Hooked on Horror III.* Westport, CT: Libraries Unlimited, 2009.

Frolund, Tina. *Genrefied Classics: A Guide to Reading Interests in Classic Literature.* Westport, CT: Libraries Unlimited, 2006.

Gannon, Michael B. *Blood, Bedlam, Bullets, and Badguys.* Westport, CT: Libraries Unlimited, 2004.

Herald, Diana Tixier, and Bonnie Kunzel. *Fluent in Fantasy: The Next Generation.* Westport, CT: Libraries Unlimited, 2007.

Hill, Nancy Milone. *Perfectly Paranormal: A Guide to Adult and Teen Reading Interests.* Westport, CT: Libraries Unlimited, 2014.

Honig, Megan. *Urban Grit: A Guide to Street Lit.* Westport, CT: Libraries Unlimited, 2010.

Johnson, Sarah L. *Historical Fiction II.* Westport, CT: Libraries Unlimited, 2009.

Martínez, Sara E. *Latino Literature: A Guide to Reading Interests.* Westport, CT: Libraries Unlimited, 2009.

Mort, John. *Christian Fiction: A Guide to the Genre.* Westport, CT: Libraries Unlimited, 2002.

Mort, John. *Read the High Country: A Guide to Western Books and Films.* Westport, CT: Libraries Unlimited, 2006.

Niebuhr, Gary Warren. *Caught Up in Crime: A Reader's Guide to Crime Fiction and Nonfiction.* Westport, CT: Libraries Unlimited, 2009.

Niebuhr, Gary Warren. *Make Mine a Mystery II: A Readers' Guide to Mystery and Detective Fiction.* Westport, CT: Libraries Unlimited, 2011.

Orr, Cynthia, and Diana Tixier Herald, eds. *Genreflecting: A Guide to Popular Reading Interests.* 7th ed. Westport, CT: Libraries Unlimited, 2013.

Pawuk, Michael. *Graphic Novels: A Genre Guide to Comic Novels, Manga, and More.* Westport, CT: Libraries Unlimited, 2006.

Pearl, Nancy, and Sarah Statz Cords. *Now Read This III: A Guide to Mainstream Fiction.* Westport, CT: Libraries Unlimited, 2010.

Ramdell, Kirstin. *Romance Fiction: A Guide to the Genre.* 2nd ed. Westport, CT: Libraries Unlimited, 2012.

Reisner, Rosalind. *Jewish American Literature.* Westport, CT: Libraries Unlimited, 2004.

Smith, Sharron, and Maureen O'Connor. *Canadian Fiction: A Guide to Reading Interests.* Westport, CT: Libraries Unlimited, 2005.

Vnuk, Rebecca, and Nanette Donohue. *Women's Fiction: A Guide to Popular Reading Interests*. Westport, CT: Libraries Unlimited, 2013.

American Library Association Series

Bouricius, Ann. *The Romance Readers' Advisory: The Librarian's Guide to Love in the Stacks*. Chicago: American Library Association, 2000.

Buker, Derek M. *The Science Fiction and Fantasy Readers' Advisory: The Librarian's Guide to Cyborgs, Aliens, and Sorcerers*. Chicago: American Library Association, 2002.

Charles, John, Candace Clark, Joanne Hamilton-Selway, and Joanna Morrison. *The Readers' Advisory Guide to Mystery.* 2nd ed. Chicago: American Library Association, 2012.

Goldsmith, Francisca. *The Readers' Advisory Guide to Graphic Novels*. Chicago: American Library Association, 2010.

Hooper, Brad. *The Short Story Readers' Advisory: A Guide to the Best*. Chicago: American Library Association, 2000.

Morris, Vanessa Irvin. *The Readers' Advisory Guide to Street Literature*. Chicago: American Library Association, 2012.

Saricks, Joyce G. *The Readers' Advisory Guide to Genre Fiction*. 2nd ed. Chicago: American Library Association, 2009.

Spatford, Becky Siegel. *The Readers' Advisory Guide to Horror.* 2nd ed. Chicago: American Library Association, 2012.

Wyatt, Neal. *The Readers' Advisory Guide to Nonfiction*. Chicago: American Library Association, 2007.

Ziebarth, Alan. *The Readers' Advisory Guide to Science Fiction*. Chicago: American Library Association, 2014.

Read On Series

Alpert, Abby. *Read On ... Graphic Novels: Reading Lists for Every Taste*. Westport, CT: Libraries Unlimited, 2012.

Clark, Craig A., and Richard T. Fox. *Read On ... Sports: Reading Lists for Every Taste*. Westport, CT: Libraries Unlimited, 2013.

Frolund, Tina. *Read On ... History: Reading Lists for Every Taste*. Westport, CT: Libraries Unlimited, 2013.

Hollands, Neil. *Read On ... Fantasy Fiction: Reading Lists for Every Taste*. Westport, CT: Libraries Unlimited, 2007.

Hooper, Brad. *Read On ... Historical Fiction: Reading Lists for Every Taste*. Westport, CT: Libraries Unlimited, 2006.

Pulliam, June Michele, and Anthony J. Fonseca. *Read On ... Horror Fiction: Reading Lists for Every Taste*. Westport, CT: Libraries Unlimited, 2006.

Reisner, Rosalind. *Read On ... Life Stories: Reading Lists for Every Taste*. Westport, CT: Libraries Unlimited, 2009.

Roche, Rick, *Read On ... Biography: Reading Lists for Every Taste*. Westport, CT: Libraries Unlimited, 2012.

Torres-Roman, Steven A. *Read On . . . Science Fiction: Reading Lists for Every Taste*. Westport, CT: Libraries Unlimited, 2010.

Trott, Barry. *Read On . . . Crime Fiction: Reading Lists for Every Taste*. Westport, CT: Libraries Unlimited, 2007.

Vnuk, Rebecca. *Read On . . . Women's Fiction: Reading Lists for Every Taste*. Westport, CT: Libraries Unlimited, 2009.

Index

About the Editor and Contributors

MEAGAN LACY earned her BA, with majors in philosophy and English, at Seattle University; her MLIS at the University of Washington; and her MA in English at Indiana University–Purdue University Indianapolis. Her research interests include young adult readers, the social aspects of reading, and critical library instruction.

ELIZABETH BROOKBANK earned her MLIS from the University of Washington's Information School and her BA from Middlebury College. As an Instruction Librarian, she teaches information literacy skills to college students, vies for their attention on social media, and takes every opportunity she can get to encourage them to read.

EMERSON CASE earned his PhD in English, with a specialization in Teaching English to Speakers of Other Languages (TESOL) from Ball State University in 2000. His areas of research include second language acquisition theory and teaching second language writing, as well as the effective use of a common reader in FYE courses.

PAULINE DEWAN received her MLIS from the University of Western (London, Ontario), her MA in English from McMaster University (Hamilton, Ontario), and her PhD in English from York University (Toronto, Ontario). She has published two books about children's literature as well as articles about reading and academic libraries, online instruction, citation management, the future of eBooks in college libraries, and distractions in the workplace.

JULIE ELLIOTT is an Associate Reference Librarian and Coordinator of Public Relations and Outreach at Indiana University South Bend. She enjoys reading mysteries whenever she can, but with two boys under the age of three, she is also becoming very acquainted with board books and looks forward to learning a lot about children's literature in the future.

BARBARA FISTER is the author of three mysteries and a book on Third World women's literatures as well as articles on information literacy, reading in popular culture, and the future of publishing. She is a regular contributor to *Library Journal* and *Inside Higher Ed* and is currently studying reading communities online.

KAREN HANSEN earned her MLIS from the University of Illinois at Urbana-Champaign in 2005 and has served in public libraries for the past eight years. In addition to leading the Mission Impossible program for three years, she has also focused on digital books, social media, and going green.

HAROLD HENKEL holds a BA in classics from University of Rochester, an MSLS from Catholic University, and an MBA from Regent University. His research interests include online library instruction, moral leadership, and community reading programs.

REBECCA MALINOWSKI is currently Special Projects Coordinator for SWAN, a membership organization for libraries in Chicagoland to house their collections and data in a shared, collaborative environment. Rebecca was previously a librarian and readers' advisor at the Oak Park (Illinois) Public Library and serves on the steering committee of the Chicago area Adult Reading Roundtable.

WILLIE MILLER is a 2010 graduate of the Indiana University School of Library & Information Science, an Indiana's Librarians Leading in Diversity Scholar, and a 2012 American Library Association Emerging Leader. His research focuses on library outreach and marketing, instructional technology, and library instruction.

SARAH FAY PHILIPS began her career as the Outreach and First-Year Experience Librarian at California State University, Bakersfield. She continues to create and implement innovative programs that make the University Library an essential part of the student experience across majors and disciplines as the Instructional Services Librarian and Assessment Coordinator at the Humboldt State University Library.

LESLEY WILLIAMS has been Head of Adult Services at the Evanston Public Library for the past 18 years. She has lead Mission Impossible for the past 5 years and also leads the African American Literature discussion group. She recently initiated "11 Months of African American History," a yearlong series of play readings, book and movie discussions, and speakers.

Edwards Brothers Malloy
Ann Arbor MI. USA
May 28, 2015